Rees Gronow

Captain Gronow's last recollections

Being the fourth and final series of his reminiscences and anecdotes. Second

Edition

Rees Gronow

Captain Gronow's last recollections
Being the fourth and final series of his reminiscences and anecdotes. Second Edition

ISBN/EAN: 9783337173838

Printed in Europe, USA, Canada, Australia, Japan

Cover: Foto ©Andreas Hilbeck / pixelio.de

More available books at **www.hansebooks.com**

CAPTAIN GRONOW'S

LAST RECOLLECTIONS;

BEING THE

FOURTH AND FINAL SERIES

OF HIS

REMINISCENCES AND ANECDOTES.

With a Portrait.

SECOND EDITION.

LONDON:
SMITH, ELDER & CO., 65 CORNHILL.
1866.

ADVERTISEMENT.

WHILE the proofs of this volume were in the hands of Captain Gronow for final revision, the publishers were surprised and concerned at hearing the unexpected news of his death.

Captain Gronow's recollections of his career—as an Eton boy, as an officer in the Guards, with which he served in the Peninsula and at Waterloo, and as member for Stafford in the first Reformed Parliament—and his varied experiences of fashionable life and high society both in Paris and London, have been recorded in successive volumes of anecdotes, of which this is the fourth and last.

Nothing further, therefore, need be recorded of

his long and exciting life, than that he was descended from an ancient Welsh family in Glamorganshire, and received his commission in the Guards at the age of eighteen, and that he died in Paris on the 20th of November 1865, in his seventy-second year.

Referring to the present volume, Captain Gronow wrote, sadly, a few weeks before his death:—" I have lived long enough to have lost all my dearest and best friends. The great laws of humanity have left me on a high and dry elevation, from which I am doomed to look over a sort of Necropolis, whence it is my delight to call forth certain choice spirits of the past."

It will be gratifying to his readers to know, that while Captain Gronow's latter years were occupied in recording these reminiscences, they were also cheered by the society of his wife and family.

CONTENTS.

CAPTAIN GRONOW'S

LAST RECOLLECTIONS.

CAMP LIFE DURING THE PENINSULAR WAR.—
There was a wide difference in the camp life of the
English and French armies.

An English soldier in camp appeared to be the
most uncomfortable of mortals; there was no plan
laid down for his recreation, or the employment of
his leisure hours, and you might see him either
brushing his clothes or cleaning his accoutrements,
or else sitting on his knapsack, smoking his pipe to
pass the time. We had no large tent wherein the
men could congregate to converse, read, or otherwise amuse themselves, and when the weather was
wet, they huddled together in small tents, where the
atmosphere was worse than that of the Black Hole
of Calcutta. The pipeclay system of tormenting
our men, by requiring them to keep their kits clean,

A

and punishing them by extra drills if the firelock or belts were not as spotless as on parade at the Horse Guards, was (to say the least of it) extremely injudicious.

The French soldiers, on the other hand, had small tents, amply large enough for five or six men, or, in default of these, they constructed tents with earth, trees, and rushes. Streets were formed, with squares; places of amusement were planned, and large trenches were dug in every direction, to drain the ground thoroughly. The officers, if near a town, took possession of the best lodgings, for the convenience of coffee-houses and kitchens; but, although they had every luxury they could afford or procure, their motto was, "*À la guerre comme la guerre.*" On entering a French camp you saw as much order as in the best regulated towns. Gendarmes kept strict watch over the soldiers, a fire-brigade was always in readiness, and everything was arranged methodically. The dress of the French soldier was not only loose and comfortable, but easily cleaned, and his knapsack was remarkable for its convenience. A *cantinière* was attached to the camp, and supplied the officers and men with wine and spirits according to regulations.

The French soldier marched quicker than the English, both in advance and retreat; and after a victory by our troops few prisoners were taken. The Duke of Wellington, with all his wonderful foresight and genius, could never get at the secret why so few stragglers were met with in following the enemy; whereas at Burgos, after our raising the siege of that town, indescribable confusion arose, and nearly half the English army were either left behind or taken prisoners by Soult and Clauzel.

The system of outposts in the French army was on a different footing from ours. Before the enemy, the French sentinel was relieved every hour; whereas our soldiers remained on duty two hours!— the extra hour caused great fatigue, and in cold weather induced sleep. A troop of the 11th Light Dragoons on duty in front—that is, at the extreme vedette, in the immediate presence of the enemy— was once caught napping. The French officer in command, observing the bad guard kept, ordered forward a sergeant and five men, who entered our lines and found Captain Wood and his men fast asleep; when the dragoons awoke, they were compelled to surrender themselves prisoners of war. Now, if the vedette had been changed every hour, this disgraceful catastrophe would not have occurred. Doubtless all these matters are better arranged now : the Crimean war ought to have taught us many valuable lessons, and our experience, so dearly bought, should be made profitable for the future. Were we to take a leaf out of the French book of tactics, instead of following the German school in all its pedantries, our armies would be better prepared for active service than they now are.

I may here mention an incident which befell Captain George Mansel, R.N., who related it to me. He was deputed by the Duke of Wellington to accompany the French army, under Marshal Clauzel, to the siege of Constantine. The expedition proved a failure, owing to causes which it is superfluous to mention ; the French army raised the siege, and commenced a most disastrous retreat. It happened that Mansel on one occasion slept in the tent occupied by the commanding-officer of the Engineers, who showed our countryman every possible attention. This French officer was rather loquacious, and among other things he said that the defence of Burgos had been intrusted to him by General Clauzel when it was attacked by the army of Wellington, and that the British army had been foiled on that occasion. Mansel, like a brave and gallant Englishman, defended the honour of the British arms, and at the same time begged to know the causes that led to the disaster. The French officer replied, " I have seen a great deal of English soldiers, and better and finer troops do not exist ; with the exception of your Engineers, whom I consider the worst of any troops I have ever met with. It was to them your defeat before Burgos was owing."

When Captain Mansel returned home, he was invited by Lord Bute to pass some days with him, and to meet the Duke of Wellington. The Duke naturally asked the gallant Captain several questions respecting the retreat, and said, " Clauzel is the best general, perhaps, that the French have ; I never, during the period he commanded the French army, caught him napping." Captain Mansel then requested permission to relate what had occurred in the tent of the commanding-officer of Engineers. " By all means let us hear it," replied the Duke. Captain M. then stated what the French officer had said ; when his Grace observed, " There is some truth in what the Frenchman asserted ; but it was not entirely the fault of our Engineers. We were almost destitute of siege-cannon at Burgos ; we had few tools, and many things requisite for a siege were wanting.   It is true that the officer who commanded the artillery in the rear was removed from his post, but Captain Dixon, who succeeded him, proved a good officer : a stoppage of communications necessitated our retreat."

The great Duke was in this, as in most cases, correct.   Had he acted on his own responsibility, the siege of Burgos would never have been attempted ; or would have been attempted with proper tools, at a later period, and under more favourable circumstances.

A FORAGING PARTY ON THE ADOUR.—Early in the spring of 1814 I was ordered to proceed with Lord James Hay on a foraging expedition.   Our party consisted of fifty men, armed with firelocks, and mounted upon mules.   It would be impossible to give any adequate idea of our zigzag march and our wanderings in the dark ; at last, after proceeding in tolerably good order for about nine hours, we came in sight of a village called Dax, consisting of a few pretty houses, about a mile distant.   At break of day, wanting our accustomed breakfast, we determined to seek quarters there ; but gave directions to the non-commissioned officers to prevent the slightest disorder or pillage. My batman, Proyd, who spoke nearly every European language, advanced into the market-place with a saucepan, which he had brought with him from camp, and began striking it with a thick stick with all his might. The noise awoke the inhabitants, some of whom approached our party, and, after much persuasion, one of them was prevailed upon by Lord James to show us the Mayor's house ; and presently this personage, " dressed in a little brief authority," made his appearance. We told him that one object of our coming was to procure provisions for ourselves, and forage for our horses and mules, but that everything supplied should be paid for. The Mayor regarded us with suspicion, until Proyd entered with our teacups and boiling water, and asked in good French for some plates for " my lord." The title of " my lord " electrified the Mayor, and in less than a quarter of an hour the whole of his family appeared, and offered us and our men everything that we required.

With a heart full of thankfulness I sat down to an excellent breakfast of cold meat, eggs, coffee, and bread and butter ; and, to crown all, one of the daughters of the Mayor, an extremely elegant young lady, entered the room with some delicious comfitures, of which she said her mother begged our acceptance. The wife of the Mayor soon after joined us, and, to our astonishment and delight, began conversing with us in English. She said that she had been brought up in England, and that her mother was English, but had left her native land for France when she was about sixteen.

Having refreshed ourselves, and seen that the horses and mules had been properly groomed and baited, we gave orders to return, and our troop put itself again in motion ; the animals being laden with straw, Indian corn, and forage of every description, for which we paid the Mayor in Spanish dollars. After we had marched some hours, finding that, hampered as we were, we could not march well in the dark, we determined to halt at the first village we fell in with, and continue our march the next morning to Bayonne ; whence we were then about eight leagues distant. We soon struck a little bourg about two leagues from Dax, but could see no one stirring in the place : in fact, it seemed deserted. However, Proyd, ever alert, heard a dog bark in one of the houses, a sign that the inhabitants were hiding. We knocked first at one house and then at

another, until our patience began to be exhausted ;
when a sleepy-looking fellow popped his head out of
a window and asked us in a most insolent manner
what we wanted. While we were parleying with
him, one of the sergeants, an active young fellow,
scrambled up to the window from whence this
Caliban was jeering at us, bolted down the stairs,
opened the front door, and admitted us into the
house. It turned out to be the cabaret of the village, and it was the landlord who had just greeted us
in this abusive manner. He was evidently an inveterate enemy of the British, for he would neither
give us any information as to how our men were
to be billeted, nor show us even common civility.
However, finding our host so contumacious, we
ordered him to be placed in durance vile, determin-
ing to carry him off to head-quarters as a prisoner.

The next morning a council of war was held to
devise a plan for transporting our prisoner. Proyd,
the Figaro of the party, suggested placing him upon
a mule ; but the question was, how to get him
mounted on the back of one at so early an hour in
the morning, without creating a disturbance in the
village. Hay, however, had no scruples on that
score, and gave instructions to have the prisoner

tied upon one of the animals. Proyd, approaching the fellow from behind, threw one of the regimental bags over his head, and with the aid of his comrades fastened him securely on a mule. When all was arranged to our satisfaction, the man began to bellow, and his neighbour, finding we were in earnest, came out and begged for mercy; but to no purpose, for we were determined to make an example of the disobliging brute: so off we started with our prisoner.

We arrived in camp just in time to report the result of our expedition to the commanding-officer, who was much amused at our bringing, in addition to an ample supply of forage, &c., an impertinent fellow, with his head tied up in a bag. The next morning, after a severe lecture, our prisoner received his *congé*, and was desired to return home and tell his friends that we differed entirely from other soldiers who had occupied the country, for we paid ready money for everything we required and expected to be treated with civility by the inhabitants.

A few days afterwards, another foraging party was organised, and on their arrival at the same village every door was opened, and provisions, corn, hay, &c., offered in abundance, while the greatest civility was paid to our men. The proprietor of the inn was foremost in proffering his services, and expressed his regret for what had occurred before, stating that the cause of it was that, in the dark, the inhabitants mistaking us for a body of men belonging to the Spanish army, had fled ; as a party of soldiers belonging to that nation had a short time before robbed them of their pigs, poultry, and linen, and ill-treated their wives and daughters. After this, our soldiers, when on foraging expeditions, were ordered to dress in uniform, to show the country-people that they belonged to the British army.

GENERAL SIR WARREN PEACOCKE, GOVERNOR OF LISBON.—During the British occupation, the Governor of Lisbon was Sir Warren Peacocke, a soldier who enjoyed the utmost confidence of the Duke of Wellington. This officer was born in 1776, and when at school was given a company in a regiment his uncle had raised. He subsequently entered the Coldstream Guards, and was at the time of his death one of the oldest general officers in the British army. While at Lisbon, his duties were arduous in the extreme. He had to reconcile the Portuguese Government and authorities to a military occupation, which they always looked upon with

suspicion ; and he had to control and direct all
the transport service of the navy : but his most
onerous labours were in connexion with the many
questions arising with regard to the army.   Lisbon,
at the period to which I refer, was a sort of hospital
for the army of the Peninsula, whilst it was at the
same time the basis of those glorious operations
the effect of which was to drive the French out of
Spain, and General Peacocke was referred to on all
occasions by the Portuguese and English.

No small part of his duties consisted in dealing
with the friends and relations of officers in our army,
a crowd of whom came over from England, each
with a special object in view.   Some wanted a
prolongation of leave for a son or brother ; others
that their friends or relations might be permitted
to return to England on account of urgent domestic
affairs ; while with the rest the excuse was, that ill
health, owing to change of climate, ought to influence the Governor to permit some stalwart soldier
to visit his native land.   To all these importuni-
ties Sir Warren was wont to reply, that " he could
not, on any account, permit domestic affairs to
interfere with the duties of the service."   Whilst

tormented with these petty annoyances, he was constantly engaged in the most important correspondence with the British Government, the Duke of Wellington, and the Portuguese officials. Many of the services he rendered his country at that time were such as cannot be transferred to the pages of history, being of the most delicate and confidential character. Throughout all, Sir Warren was remarkable for his urbanity of manner, his untiring business habits, and a keen judgment, which made him alike an accomplished statesman and an intelligent soldier.

Some of the complaints made to the gallant officer were frivolous in the extreme. On one occasion an assistant-surgeon complained, in no measured terms, of the quarters allotted to him, stating that he was obliged to sleep in a pigsty ; upon which Sir Warren inquired of one of his subalterns if he knew anything of the said pigsty. The answer was, that the quarters which the surgeon complained of were very good, in fact, better than the majority of the officers occupied. " Oh, then, sir," said Peacocke, turning to the injured medico, " if you are a prince in disguise, declare yourself ; but if you are only what your diploma states you to be, I consider the quarters you have quite good enough."

Lisbon, owing to the continental war then raging, was the only port open to the English, and thither our countrymen and women flocked ; in fact, Lisbon was then what Paris and Rome are now, and some of our most celebrated men show there to advantage. It was there that the immortal poet Byron first touched foreign soil, and where some of his daring, powerful poetry was written ; he became the idol of the women, and the lionising he underwent there might have made him exceedingly vain, for he was admired wherever he went. His favourite resort was the opera, where most of the young men of fashion in Lisbon congregated in the evening. He was generally accompanied by his friends, Dan Mackinnon, Hervey Aston, Colin Campbell, and William Burrell. The opera at Lisbon was its chief attraction, and it was there that the celebrated singers, Catalini, Collini, Naldi, and Ambrogetti, with Presle, Angiolini, Deshayes, and the rest of the *corps de ballet* riveted the attention of hearers and beholders ; and thence those artistes were engaged for the London Operahouse.

Byron well describes these " amusing vagabonds," as he calls them, and their English admirers :—

> " Well may the nobles of our present race
> Watch each distortion of a Naldi's face !
> Well may they smile on Italy's buffoons,
> And worship Catalini's pantaloons.
>
> . . . .
>
> While Gayton bounds before the enraptured looks
> Of hoary marquises and stripling dukes,
> Let high-born ladies eye the lively Presle
> Twirl her light limbs and spurn the heedless veil ;
> Let Angiolini bare her breast of snow,
> Wave the white arm, and point the pliant toe ;
> Collini trill her love-inspiring song,
> Strain her fair neck, and charm the listening throng."

During the war, Colonel Gould, the factotum of the English ladies patronesses, and manager of her Majesty's Theatre in London, went once a year to Lisbon to hire his *troupe ;* as Waters, Ebers, Laporte, and others, subsequently went to Paris and engaged singers and dancers.

I have been informed that the Duke of Wellington, during the Peninsular War, visited Lisbon only once, remaining three days at that town, at the Palace of Necessidades ; and on this occasion he was received in the most enthusiastic manner by the Portuguese and English. Unfortunately, Marshal Beresford and our Minister, Sir Charles Stuart, afterwards Lord Stuart de Rothsay, were at this time at variance, and hated each other most cordially. The Marshal wanted to lodge our great commander at his own house, and thereby monopolise his society ; but to no purpose, as the Duke went to the palace. The Duke did not disguise his displeasure at the inefficiency exhibited by many of the superior officers in the British army then at Lisbon, and sent several of them back to England, saying, " It is not my fault that they are sent home, but the fault of those who sent them out."

Whilst the Duke was insisting on Sir Warren Peacocke's acting with severity against the skulkers from the army, these gentlemen were complaining bitterly of the Governor for not allowing them to shirk their duties, alleging that, on account of " ill health," (unfortunately a common excuse in the service,) they ought to be allowed to remain at Lisbon to recruit it : this " recruiting of health," be it understood, generally consisting of a minimum of work, combined with a maximum of dissipation. Sir Warren was so disgusted with the amount of extra work and anxiety entailed upon him by these useless officers, that he several times requested the Duke to find some one to supply his place as Governor ; but the answer he generally received was, " You are too valuable here to be replaced by any one. I cannot possibly spare you."

FRANK RUSSELL AT THE BATTLE OF THE PYRE-NEES.—After the battle of Vittoria our army marched to the Pyrenees, where took place those operations in the passes, and that brilliant succession of victories, which have given historical character to the names of Picton, Lowry Cole, Adam, Colville, and a hundred others. At that time nothing was thought impossible for British soldiers; after those victories the French soldiers were not to be compared with the English, although our adversaries were commanded by Soult. From Torres Vedras to the Bidassoa we carried everything before us, and we were only momentarily checked at the battle of the Pyrenees, where Lord Wellington found that the French were not disposed to allow us to invade their country without a severe struggle. At that memorable battle, Soult made a desperate effort to drive us back again into Spain ; but he found to his cost that the fiercer he fought the more desperate was the resistance he had to encounter, till at length he

B

saw it was impossible to withstand our invincible
phalanx.

One of the heroes of that bloody day was Frank
Russell, " the Pride of Woburn Abbey," whose character it would be as difficult to overestimate as it
would be to give an idea of his chivalrous bearing
in presence of the enemy.   He possessed all the
requisites for a good soldier.   Of noble birth, good
looking, and with a splendid figure, he was valiant
in the extreme.   He was gazetted in the 7th
Fusiliers at the age of sixteen, and forthwith sent
with them to Spain, where he followed the fortunes
of his corps up to the time of the battle of the
Pyrenees.   One of the most furious attacks made
by Soult on our position at this celebrated conflict
was directed on the left wing of the British army.
The Fusiliers were posted on the right, and
ordered to maintain themselves against all odds,
and not to budge a foot.   The French General being
determined to turn our right, sent an overwhelming
force against Frank's regiment, which was posted
against a mountain wall.   The Fusiliers defended
themselves with obstinate courage, but their Colonel,
for some reason which was never explained, declared
it prudent to order a retreat, though his line was

unbroken. Frank Russell, however, shouted out, " Not yet, Colonel," and with the colours of his regiment mounted the wall and cheered our men on ; the French meanwhile renewing their attack with redoubled vigour. During this fierce struggle, however, our hero kept his position, till the fierce energy with which the French had been fighting began to cool : for Wellington had meanwhile broken Soult's centre, and the retreat of the French forces was ordered. Before Russell quitted his post of honour, Lord Wellington with his staff happened to pass by the wall, and saw Russell standing on the wall, holding the colours of his regiment, which were riddled with bullet holes. On the following day, when the gallant young officer's conduct was reported to our great commander, he exclaimed, " Ah ! there's nothing like blood."

The chivalrous bearing of Frank Russell affords a memorable example of the feeling which actuated young officers at the time of which I am now speaking. As a man of the world, Frank was a great favourite with the fair sex, and enjoyed in a remarkable degree the confidence of his friends ; for his temper and disposition were eminently sociable, and he was noted for his kindness of heart. He died at an early age, holding a company of the Guards, and was universally regretted. A pretty compliment was paid to him by the Duchess of York, who presented him with a ring, made by Lawrier, the jeweller in St James's Street, having for a motto, "None but the brave deserve the fair."

HUNTING IN THE PYRENEES, 1813, 1814.—The Commissary-General, Marsden, who belonged to head-quarters, succeeded in collecting from England a kennel of splendid hounds. On the Marquis of Worcester's (the late Duke of Beaufort) leaving the army, he promised to send some of his father's dogs to Marsden ; other gentlemen followed this nobleman's example, and before we crossed the Bidassoa the pack was complete, and in fine condition. The hunting in the Pyrenees reminded me of my native Wales ; it was all up hill and down dale, and for that reason, when a fox was found he was seldom if ever killed. The best riders belonging to the hunt were the officers of the 14th and 16th Dragoons, who were, as a rule, well mounted. I have seen at a meet in the Pyrenees about two hundred officers assembled, some (as I have said) well mounted, but the majority on " screws," ponies, or even mules—a strange contrast to the Quorn and Pytchley gatherings. The greatest character of all was Lascelles, on his immense horse, on which he used to delight to race up hill for a lark; and many were the scrapes he got into with the whipper-in for riding over the bounds.

One fine morning in October 1813, Reynard took it into his head to cross the Bidassoa, and the dogs and huntsman, heedless of danger, followed. The notes of the hounds and the cheering of the huntsman alarmed a French drum-major and some twenty boys whom he was instructing in a secluded spot on the banks of the river. Instead of showing fight, the drum-major with his young pupils scampered off; the dogs meanwhile, accompanied by the huntsman, were in full cry, and shortly afterwards killed a fine dog fox. The field had remained on our side of the river, enjoying the sport without incurring any danger; when all of a sudden the enemy, wondering what the deuce we were about, came down in force, with a battery of field-pieces, and opened fire, which made us all scamper off as if old Nick had been at our heels. Marsden, however, advanced to the water's edge, and with his white pocket handkerchief as a flag of truce, asked permission of the French officer in command to cross and explain what we were doing. This request was acceded to, and when our gallant foe had heard the reasons why we had advanced out of bounds, he very graciously permitted the huntsman and dogs to recross the river and join us.

DYSENTERY IN THE PENINSULA.—Early in the year 1812 the Duke of York despatched to the seat of war the 3d Battalion of my old regiment. It was considered by military men to have been the finest in his Majesty's service. All the men, with the exception of the grenadier company, were strong, active young fellows, but had not seen active service. They were conveyed to Cadiz, in men-of-war, and arrived there without any accident; but owing to change of diet, and the substituting the horrid wine of the country for the porter they had been accustomed to at home, before the expiration of a few weeks, five hundred of these fine fellows died in the hospital at Vizu, and were buried in the church-yard there. I mention this to show how careful commanding-officers ought to be to prevent similar consequences from decimating bodies of fresh troops: although warnings of this sort have occurred all over the globe.

On joining my regiment in the Peninsula, one of the grenadiers, a tall and well-built man, was recommended to me as the best person to employ for pitching my tent. This man had been brought up as a carpenter, but through some misunderstanding with his relations had enlisted. While cutting the trench he entered into conversation with me, and said he hoped, as I appeared very young and unaccustomed to bivouacking, that I would forgive him for being so bold as to offer a little salutary advice : which was, to drink every morning on rising a small glass of brandy or rum, as by so doing rheumatism, dysentery, and many other camp disorders, would be prevented. He added, with tears in his eyes, that he had lost his brother at Vizu, owing to his not following the advice he was now giving me. I was so struck with the earnest manner of the man that I adopted his panacea, and during the whole time that I was in camp I never had a day's illness.

A DARING EXPLOIT.—Among the incidents that occurred in the war in Spain, the following will no doubt surprise the reader :—In Picton's division in the Pyrenees, there was an Irishman of extraordinary courage, by name O'Keefe, who was addicted to all sorts of irregularities, which brought him more than once to the halberds, but who performed a feat worthy of the heroes of antiquity. Near the pass of Ronces-valles the French occupied a peak or impregnable mountain called the Boar's Head, at the top of which a company of the enemy was posted. To drive them away appeared impossible ; Picton thought so, and determined to invest this natural fort, to prevent useless bloodshed. During a reconnaissance, the Gene-ral said, in a loud voice, which was overheard by the men below, that the French could, if they pleased, pelt us away with stones from the top of the moun-tain. O'Keefe stepped up, touched his cap, and addressed Sir T. Picton thus : "If your honour chooses, I will take the hill alone." This speech asto-nished all who heard it ; but not the General, who had frequently witnessed the daring and intrepidity of O'Keefe. "If you do so," replied Sir Thomas, " I will report it to Lord Wellington, and I promise you your discharge, with a shilling a day for life." O'Keefe stole away, having whispered to the com-manding-officer of his company to follow him, and climbed up the goat path, the English sentinels fir-ing at him, thinking he was deserting to the enemy. O'Keefe having entered the stronghold of the French, was received with open arms, as a deserter. He then began to play his part, by showing signs of imbecility, laughing, dancing, singing, &c.; so that the enemy thought that they had actually received a madman instead of a deserter, and told him to decamp, as there was not food enough there to feed him. During this farce, our men quickly got up to the summit, where they found O'Keefe occupying the attention of the enemy. They rushed in and took possession of this stronghold without losing a man. O'Keefe (I believe that was his name) received for this act of daring the nomination of one of the warders of the Tower from the Duke of Wellington.

My Soldier-Servant.—When in Spain with my regiment, it fell to my lot to receive from the ranks a soldier born in Sicily, of Sicilian parentage, by name Proyd. When the Guards occupied Catania, this individual, having lost his father and mother, was adopted by the regiment, and through the instrumentality of Lord Proby, became a soldier, and was inscribed on the muster-roll of the 1st Foot Guards. He was an excellent servant, and perhaps the best caterer in the army; for when we were in-

vading the Pyrenees, he supplied me with every deli-
cacy, while the army generally was living on salt beef
and biscuits : in fact, poultry, mutton, and fresh
bread at my table were the rule, rather than the
exception.　With all these accomplishments, he possessed one fault—a too great admiration, unqualified
with respect, for the charms of the fair sex, and he
seldom lost an opportunity of stealing a kiss from
any pretty girl that came in his way.

On our return from the Peninsula, I took this
Figaro with me to White Knights, the seat of the
Duke of Marlborough, where I was invited to spend
some days.　At this charming house I found a great
number of visitors, among whom were Lord and
Lady Grenville, Lord and Lady Macclesfield, Mr
Mathias, the author of the "Pursuits of Literature,"
Lord William Fitzroy, Mr Garlick, and others.　It
happened on the day of my arrival that my servant
met the maid of Lady Macclesfield on the staircase,
and without the slightest ceremony he attempted to
kiss her.　The maid, unaccustomed to such behaviour,
screamed, ran down stairs, and then up again, with
Proyd close at her heels ; he even followed her into
her lady's room, where she flew to take refuge.　Her
ladyship, alarmed at seeing a strange man in her room,

shrieked loudly; many persons ran to her assistance; and her noble husband, more dead than alive, thinking some sad disaster had befallen the Countess, inquired with caution, " What is the matter ?" Her ladyship replied in a faint voice, " The man is under the bed." Pokers and tongs were seized, and the noble Lord made use of his weapons to such purpose that the delinquent quietly surrendered. This incident, which created great confusion, rendered it necessary that the Sicilian should be sent to rejoin his regiment. Poor Proyd soon after applied for his discharge, and returned to his native land to make love to his own countrywomen.

SIR THOMAS STYLES.—Poor Sir Thomas Styles, who fought with the poet Shelley at Eton, received a commission in the 1st Foot Guards. Had it been in the time of peace, poor Styles would have shone to advantage on parade and at the mess-table ; but the active life of a soldier proved too fatiguing for him, as will be seen by the following anecdote. In course of time he was sent with a detach- ment of his regiment to Portugal ; but on his arrival at Lisbon, the Guards had left to join the army in the neighbourhood of the Pyrenees ; ac-

cordingly, our young Guardsman received orders to
march through Portugal and Spain until he came
up with his regiment. The heat was excessive;
and on his falling in with the brigade, poor Styles
was more dead than alive. All his brother officers
hastened to congratulate him on his safe arrival
after so long a march; but he spoke little, saying,
that, ever since he had left Lisbon, he had not
closed his eyes for half-an-hour, and that his health
was in such a state that he feared he could not long
survive. Observing that something extraordinary
had happened, he was pressed to be more explicit,
and to tell what had occurred to make him so
miserable. He replied, with a very grave countenance, that the fleas and vermin on the march had
nearly driven him mad; and that when the peasant
girls observed him scratching himself, they would
laugh, and shaking their petticoats over pails full
of water, tell him how much more they were to be
pitied than he. Our doctor, Mr Bacot, a very kind
fellow, anticipating brain fever, placed Styles in his
camp bed, covered his head with wet towels, and
desired his batman to watch over his master, and
not to leave him for an instant. However, the
servant fell asleep, and during the night poor Styles

got out of bed, unlocked his trunk where his razors were kept, and with one of them deliberately cut his throat from ear to ear.

SIR JOHN ELLEY OF THE "BLUES."—In my former volumes I have had the pleasure of relating several anecdotes of this gallant officer; and in the third volume, I mentioned his having commenced his military career as a private in the Blues. I have received a letter from a gentleman, who knew him personally, giving me the following information respecting this dashing hero:—"I spent some time at Harrowgate with this gallant soldier, whom I admired not only for his bravery, but for his talents; he was replete with wit and fun, and full of the most interesting anecdotes. On my leaving him, he said that he had an old acquaintance residing not far from my father's place, whither I was going, and he would feel obliged if I would ride over some day to a certain toll-bar in the west of Cumberland, and deliver a message to his old friend, the sergeant who had enlisted him in the Blues. I did not forget a promise which might lead to some anecdotes respecting Sir John's early life; and shortly after arriving at home, I mounted my nag, rode to the toll-bar, and saw the old sergeant, who kept the turnpike and appeared to be seventy-five years of age. When he came to take the toll, he appeared much astonished at receiving the message from Sir John, and asking after his health said, that it was true that he had enlisted him into the Blues, and he related the circumstance :—' The sergeant having charge of a recruiting party at Barnet, one fine day a tall and respectable-looking young fellow addressed him, stating he wanted to enlist ; the shilling was therefore given, and on the following day the recruit was sent to head-quarters, where he was passed and duly enlisted in the Royal Guards.'

The old man being asked what he knew of Sir John's antecedents said, that the appearance and manner of the recruit proved him to have been a gentleman. He declined affirming as to the truth of what he had heard ; but added that the report current in the regiment after his entering it, was that the new recruit had held a cornet's commission in the Scots Greys, then quartered at Doncaster ; but owing to a misunderstanding with an officer about a lady, he had thrown up his commission in disgust, and having spent all his money, enlisted as a private in the manner described. In the barrack-room he was hail fellow well met with all his comrades, who nevertheless treated him as their superior. As a swordsman and rider, he was considered the best in the regiment ; and in consequence of his gentlemanly deportment, and being a good penman, he was taken into the adjutant's office, whence he was promoted to a commission in the regiment.

Perhaps the most distinguished service ever performed by Sir John Elley was in the cavalry engagement at the battle of Vittoria, when he was assistant adjutant-general to the cavalry under the immediate command of Sir W. Cotton. Sir William had given directions to the 3d Light Dragoons to charge a superior force of the enemy, which proved disastrous ; for the regiment was almost entirely cut to pieces. Sir John Elley observing this disaster, got together as many of the 14th and 16th Dragoons as he could, and charged at the head of them through the enemy ; thereby saving many of the fine fellows who were dispersed and unable to act. In the charge he was knocked down, together with his horse, the fall breaking his leg ; and although continually ridden over by friend and foe in the *mêlée*, Elley, nothing daunted, cheered on his men to fight for the honour of old England, and at last, catching hold of Sergeant Cooper's stirrup, was dragged to the rear.

JACK TALBOT OF THE GUARDS.—Poor Jack Talbot, after leaving Eton, entered the Coldstream Guards, and accompanied his regiment to Spain, where he evinced great courage, and was foremost in every fight. Though he possessed many imperfections, he was the manliest and kindest of human beings, and was the idol of the women ; and their champion, also, for he was one of the few men who would never hear improper epithets applied to them under any circumstances, or allow their failings to be criticised by those who were in all probability the cause of them.   There was a charm in Talbot's conversation that I never found in that of any other man ; his brave good heart, and love of punch, made him an agreeable companion, and many friends.   When in his cups, or rather bowls, he would talk facetiously about his rich father in Ireland, Lord Malahide, spending that nobleman's money all the time.   He was foolishly generous.   I have often seen him, at a club or in a coffee-house, pay for the whole of his friends present ; and his liberality to women of all classes was profuse.   He used to say, " I would rather disoblige my father or my best friend than a pretty woman."

Whether in the Guards' club or at private assemblies, you were always sure to find Jack surrounded by a circle of friends, amused with his witty conversation and charmed with his good humour. He had always a smile on his face ; in fact, everybody acknowledged him as their friend, from Beau Brummel to Theodore Hook.

During his last illness, Alvanley asked the doctor of the regiment what he thought of it. The doctor replied, " My Lord, he is in a bad way, for I was obliged to make use of the lancet this morning." " You should have tapped him, doctor," said Lord Alvanley ; " for I am sure he has more claret than blood in his veins." The late Duke of Beaufort one day called upon him at his lodgings in Mount Street, and found him drinking sherry at breakfast : the duke remonstrated with him, saying, " It will be the death of you." Talbot replied, " I get drunk every night, and find myself the better for it next morning." Talbot was a great favourite of the late Duke of Cambridge, who frequently called to inquire after his health. Upon one occasion, the captain's servant, in answer to the Duke's interroga-

tions, told His Royal Highness that his master did
not want to see either doctor or parson, but only
wished to be left to die in peace. The Duke, with
sad forebodings, sent Dr Keate to see him; the
doctor, on his arrival, found Talbot seated in his
arm-chair dead, with a bottle of sherry half-empty
on the table beside him. He was only twenty-seven.

"TEAPOT" CRAWFURD.—Crawfurd was brought
up at Eton, and subsequently entered the 10th
Hussars. He possessed immense strength, was a
handsome fellow, and his bravery was proverbial.
His riding to hounds particularly, when a boy at
Melton Mowbray and Belvoir Castle, was plucky
in the extreme. He was called "Teapot," because
of his predilection when at Eton for brewing tea
in a black pot, which he kept and cherished when
a soldier; though some would have it that his
handsome head looked like those on old-fashioned
teapots. He was noble-looking to the last day of
his life, though worn down by disease. As a companion, he was charming; his bewitching manner
found him friends everywhere, and he was courted
by the dandies and men of fashion. He married
Lady Barbara Coventry, a very beautiful woman,

with whom he lived happily many years. The Prince Regent was very partial to him ; and on the occasion of the 10th Hussars being paraded before their departure for Spain, the Prince said to him, " Go, my boy, and show the world what stuff you are made of. You possess strength, youth, and courage ; go, and conquer." Crawfurd arrived in Spain, and his first rencontre with the enemy was at Orthes, where he was foremost in the charge, and behaved splendidly. A brother of his, equally brave, was killed at Waterloo, whilst defending the château of Hougomont.

THE GUARDS' CLUB.—In order that my readers may understand what I am about to relate, it is desirable for me to advert to the causes which induced the officers of the Foot Guards to form their Club. Circumstances which it is unnecessary to enter into had for a long time prevented those gallant sons of Mars from carrying out the object they had in view. Unseemly broils and quarrels often took place in the room at the St James's Coffee-house, at the bottom of St James's Street, where the officers of the Guards used to congregate, and these were caused mainly by the admission of (or rather the impossibility of excluding) Irish bullies and persons of fashionable exterior but not of good birth or breeding. Consequently the officers were obliged, on the return of their regiments from the Peninsula after the disaster at Corunna, to establish a club of their own. Arrangements were made, and the Guards' Club was formed, the subscription to which was at first only £5 per annum for each member.

Among those who first patronised this new institution were the Dukes of York, Cambridge, and Gloucester, and nearly all the general and field officers then in London. The room where the meetings of the officers of the Guards used to be held at the St James's Coffee-house was a miserable little den, the floor sanded over like a tap-room now-a-days : a strange contrast to the luxurious apartments now occupied by the officers in Pall Mall ; but notwithstanding this, among the people who used to assemble might be found all the wits of the day—Brinsley Sheridan, Jekyll, Wyndham, and others, whose choice sayings over their punch and pipes would fill a volume. The rules of the new Club excluded gambling ; and from 1812 till 1821, when I left it, I cannot recollect any serious quarrel occurring among the members, who were composed of the best men England could boast of. So great was the loyalty that pervaded them, that when the trial of Queen Caroline took place, and the *Times* made use of disrespectful language towards her, that paper was, at a meeting of the Club convened by Sir Henry Hardinge, late Lord Hardinge, expelled. *Tempora mutantur et nos mutamur in illis.*

GENERAL THORNTON AND THEODORE HOOK.—On the return of the British army from Spain in 1814, the Prince Regent, desirous of rewarding the personal associates of the Duke of Wellington, decided on removing the Generals of the Guards, and giving their places to officers of the Duke's staff who ranked as Colonels. The Generals were mostly either useless and decrepit veterans, or officers whose ideas of service consisted in attending as little as possible to their regiments, and giving the balance of their time to pleasure. One of them, General Thornton, was afflicted with the idea that of all persons in the world he was the only one who understood the art of waltzing. In fact, it was quite a mania with him; and he might be seen at nearly every party of note, making himself exceedingly ridiculous by teaching young ladies to waltz : this dance having only shortly before come into fashion. Theodore Hook gave him the *sobriquet* of the "waltzing General;" this occasioned a violent altercation between them at a ball in Portman Square, where, it is said, the General received a more personal affront from Hook : which, however, the soldier did not resent according to the then received notions of honour, by calling him out. The inquiry into this affair by a committee of the other officers of the Guards, no doubt caused the sweeping change proposed by the Prince Regent ; it was found that General Thornton had been guilty of cowardice in not demanding immediate satisfaction of Hook, and he was therefore desired to quit the regiment forthwith.   His resignation, and the comments on it at the time, paved the way to the proposed changes in command ; and when Hook heard that the companies had been given to the Duke's Colonels, he said, "I rejoice to hear that they have adopted the Wellington over-alls, and discarded their inexpressibles."   These Colonels were ever after called the "Wellington over-alls."

THE HEROIC LADY WALDEGRAVE. — When the British army was about to enter France, I was struck with the beauty and attainments of the chivalrous Lady Waldegrave, who accompanied her lord throughout the war. Her conduct was the theme of the army, and she won universal praise and admiration. She was a perfect heroine.

Since the peace, I have had the honour to receive invitations to her house in the Champs-Elysées. She used to speak of her campaigns with the same energy that an old soldier would talk of battles wherein he had distinguished himself, and would tell you of the innumerable risks she had been exposed to in the several charges of cavalry which her husband had led. She felt much, she used to say, for those poor fellows who were left wounded on the ground, and her description of their sufferings was so natural and touching that it frequently brought tears into the eyes of those who heard her. The heroine was nearly taken prisoner upon one occasion; but, upon presenting her pocket-pistol at the breast of the French cavalry soldier who menaced her, he dropped his sword, and suffered her to escape.

The Countess of Waldegrave was not only young but beautiful; she had a splendid figure, and was one of the best riders I ever saw. She was not at all masculine in her style ; her voice and manner of speaking were remarkable for sweetness and grace. I cannot hope to see her like again.

COLONEL, *alias* "JEMMY," COCHRANE OF THE GUARDS.—This gentleman was, in the fullest sense of the word, fearless—in fact, he dared danger; yet, although so brave, he was an amiable and quiet man, and an enemy to every species of disorder. Looking at him, one would have thought that he was fit only for a drawing-room, as he had most delicate hands and feet; but his figure was perfect symmetry, and his strength was prodigious. He had neither vanity nor ambition, and was a firm friend to all his comrades.

Fifty years since, my lamented friend was sent to Bristol with a recruiting party of the 3d Guards. Frequent quarrels arose between the soldiers and sailors at that place; and upon one occasion he observed a mob of brutal fellows ill-treating his recruiting-sergeant. Regardless of the immense odds against him, he ran to the rescue of the sergeant, who lay bleeding on the ground, and, alone, attacked the furious mob that surrounded them. Every blow he dealt brought

one of his adversaries to the ground, till at length
they ran away right and left, leaving him master of
the field. I was told by a gentleman who arrived
on the ground a few minutes after this unequal
fight, that he saw three men unable to move, owing
to the punishment they had received:—one had his
jaw broken, another his shoulder dislocated, and
the third was so frightfully disfigured that his own
mother would not have known him.

"Jemmy" Cochrane married a lady near Bath,
where he resided many years, and died a lieutenant-
general.

MR CORNEWALL AND THE PROVOST-SERGEANT.—
A large army is accompanied, not only by the sut-
lers and others who make their living by so doing,
but by curious or scientific men, who seek to ac-
quire either materials for small talk or solid information useful to the world at large. Our army
in the Peninsula was not an exception to the prac-
tice, and many wealthy and educated men set out
from England to follow its fortunes ; but Lord
Wellington set his face against all these intruders,
with the exception of Mr Cornewall, who was favoured with his especial patronage.

This gentleman, the eldest son of the Bishop of Hereford, having letters of introduction to his Lordship, on arriving at Lisbon, provided himself with horses, &c., and, thus equipped, reached the head-quarters of the army in the Pyrenees. He was present at all the battles, down to that of Toulouse, and upon all occasions he exhibited before the enemy the greatest *sang froid.* At Toulouse Lord Wellington requested Cornewall to be more careful of his person, saying, " If you are killed or wounded, the army will not pity you ; for you are unnecessarily courting danger." " Well, my Lord," replied Cornewall, " I think the odds are in my favour now ; having up to this moment escaped being hit, I care not for what may happen."

Cornewall happened to dine at head-quarters that day, and when returning home at a late hour, he saw a soldier suspended by the neck from a pair of halberds. He naturally hastened to the spot, where he found the provost-sergeant and a few soldiers and peasants ; and, on inquiring what it all meant, the sergeant replied, " Sir, the man you see hanging there has been found guilty of robbing and ill-treating some of these poor peasants, and was sentenced to be hanged by a drum-head court-

martial, and there he is expiating his crime." Cornewall went the next morning to head-quarters,
and related to Lord Wellington what he had seen;
upon which our illustrious hero said, "Discipline
must be maintained at any cost, or my soldiers
may become a rabble of thieves." "True, my
Lord," replied Cornewall, "but the provost-marshal's
power appears to me to be too great; for he acts as
judge and executioner, without the culprit having
time to appeal for mercy." Lord Wellington replied, "My orders are peremptory on that score;
and I would recommend you to be careful not to
get into the provost-sergeant's clutches, or you will
inevitably be strung up." "Thank you, my Lord,
for the hint. I will never more trust myself within
a hundred miles of such danger; for I would rather
be riddled with the enemy's bullets than be placed
between a pair of halberds."

ARMA VIRUMQUE CANO.—Towards the close of
the continental war, viz., in 1814, the militia of
that epoch were full of military ardour. The Marquis of Buckingham, who was enormously fat, and
not unlike the pictures which are represented of
Falstaff, volunteered, in conjunction with his friend

Sir Watkin Williams Wynne, to take their regiments, the Buckinghamshire and Flintshire Militia, to the seat of war. Permission was granted them to join the Duke of Wellington's army, and off they started for Bordeaux. But they arrived "a day after the fair," for the treaty of peace had been signed by the allied sovereigns; so, as the King of France with forty thousand men

"Marched up a hill, and then marched down again,"

our patriotic warriors were obliged to retrace their steps without having fired a shot at the enemy.

Before they re-embarked for their native land, however, they took good care to impress upon the inhabitants of Bordeaux their value as soldiers, by parading their battalions with all the pomp and circumstance of war, both in the morning and at noon. Those for whose benefit this spectacle was intended never failed attending these military parades; not with the idea of gaining any hints as to evolutions, &c., but to gaze on the commanding officers, whom they denominated, " Les bœufs-gras anglais." The militia regiments appeared but a sorry sight in comparison with British veterans who had marched through Portugal and Spain, fighting a hundred battles, and afterwards remained some time at Bordeaux, where they gained the respect of the inhabitants by their orderly conduct and manly bearing. Unfortunately, too, our militiamen did not conduct themselves in a becoming manner ; for, delighted at the cheapness of the wine and brandy, and happening to be officered by men incapable of looking after them properly, when off duty they were constantly tipsy, and getting into all sorts of scrapes and broils with the inhabitants ; so much so, that their conduct was reported to the Commander-in-Chief, who ordered them home without delay.

The wine-merchants, who had not done badly during the stay of our warlike friends in Bordeaux, persuaded the Marquis and the Welsh baronet, on the eve of their departure, into buying a quantity of stuff they designated claret. Proud of their purchase, they had it carefully shipped ; and when it arrived in due course at London, it was stowed away in the cellars of Stowe and Wynstay. Orders were eventually given to have the precious liquid bottled ; but when the casks were tapped it was found that an acetous fermentation had taken place, converting the " delicate Bordeaux wine " into very bad vinegar. The two heroes, doubly disappointed of the wine they had bought and the honours they hoped to win, commenced legal proceedings against the vendors of the liquor; but they were non-suited, and had to pay costs, amounting to a considerable sum.

SIR JERRY COGHLAN. — Sir Jeremiah Coghlan's name, and the daring acts performed by him, are familiar to every naval man. Beginning life as a cabin-boy on board a trading sloop, running between Cork and Neath, Coghlan was treated by the Captain in a most inhuman manner. The brutality of this man becoming unbearable, Jerry determined on quitting the vessel at Neath, but was caught by the police, and brought before one of the magistrates of the county, a relation of the author. The boy said that, owing to the cruel conduct of his mother, he had been obliged to leave home, and went to Cork, where he was bound as cabin-boy to the master who had treated him so ill. Under these circumstances, he was allowed to leave the sloop, and obtained employment in Neath as a bricklayer's lad in the building of a few houses which were in course of erection on the Parade. Not contented

with this mode of gaining a living, he offered his
services as ordinary seaman to a captain about to
sail for Plymouth ; he was engaged, and arrived at
that port, where a terrible storm was raging. Coghlan went on shore, and found his way to the beach,
where a number of persons were assembled to look
at a large East Indiaman, which was in danger of
being wrecked. Among the crowd was Sir Edward
Pellew, afterwards Lord Exmouth, who, perceiving
that the vessel was already aground, offered a prize
to any one who should carry a rope through the
breakers to those on board. No one venturing,
Jerry thrust himself forward, stripped, tied the rope
round his waist, dashed through the waves, and
succeeded in establishing a communication between
the shore and the ship. This heroic deed won the
admiration of all who witnessed it, and among them
that of Sir Edward Pellew, who took Coghlan on
board the man-of-war that he commanded, and
made him one of his midshipmen.

In a few years Jerry was sent into the Mediterranean, where he displayed such coolness and daring
in cutting out prizes from the enemy's ports, engaging with success French vessels larger than his own,
and running into the best guarded harbours, that

the Admiralty were induced to give him his lieu-
tenancy, and the command of a sloop of war. The
exploits Coghlan performed with this small vessel
are matters of history ; and his achievements fur-
nish instances of the wonders that can be wrought
by the union of skill, presence of mind, and ener-
getic daring : qualities which have distinguished the
British navy for the last century. Coghlan's bravery
elicited many commendations in the despatches of
Lord St Vincent, the Admiral of the Fleet. In one
place the noble Lord says :—" I did not think the
gallantry of Sir Edward Hamilton and Captain
Patrick Campbell could have been rivalled, until I
read the enclosed letter from Sir Edward Pellew,
relating the great services performed by Lieutenant
Coghlan of the *Viper* cutter, which has filled me
with pride and admiration." Lord St Vincent
also addressed the following letter to Lord Spencer,
the First Lord of the Admiralty :—

"MY DEAR LORD,—I shall not trouble your Lord-
ships with a word more than is contained in the enclosed private letter from Sir Edward Pellew, on the
subject of the intrepid Coghlan, except to say (not
out of ostentation, but to prevent the city or any
body of merchants making him a present of the same

sort) that I gave him a sword of one hundred guineas' value.—Yours faithfully, ST VINCENT."

Poor Coghlan died young, owing to the wounds he had received in the service ; but some years previous to his death the quondam cabin-boy became a Knight of the Bath. I had the honour of being well acquainted with him, and can speak with pleasure of his varied attainments, extraordinary in a self-educated man, and the manly bearing he always exhibited.

LORD JERSEY AND AN OFFICER OF THE GUARDS. —When duelling was at its height in England, the most absurd pretexts were made for calling a man out. I recollect that at one of the dinners at the Thatched House in St James's Street, Mr Willis, the proprietor, in passing behind the chairs occupied by the company, was accosted by a Captain in the 3d Guards in a rather satirical manner. Mr Willis, smarting under the caustic remarks of the gallant Captain, said aloud,—" Sir, I wrote to you at the request of Lady Jersey, saying that as her Ladyship was unacquainted with you, I had been instructed to reply to your letter, by stating that the Lady Patronesses declined sending you a ticket

D

for the ball." This statement, made in a public room, greatly irritated the Captain; his friends in vain endeavoured to calm his wrath, and he sent a cartel the following day to Lord Jersey, requesting he would name his second, &c. Lord Jersey replied in a very dignified manner, saying that if all persons who did not receive tickets from his wife were to call him to account for want of courtesy on her part, he should have to make up his mind to become a target for young officers, and he therefore declined the honour of the proposed meeting.

LORD CASTLEREAGH AND SIR E. PAKENHAM.— The following incident occurred in London in 1814. When the war had terminated in the Peninsula, Sir Edward Pakenham, with his physician, Dr John Howell, arrived in England, *en route* to North America, where Sir Edward had been named by the Duke of York, Commander-in-Chief of the British forces. Before the departure of the gallant General, he had promised Lord Castlereagh to breakfast with him, and at the same time to introduce his physician to the minister. After breakfast, Lord C. inquired of the Doctor the precise place where the jugular vein was situated. Dr Howell explained it to the satisfaction of his Lordship, stating that it would be a dangerous experiment for any man to take the slightest liberty with that artery, for death would inevitably follow if it were pierced. When the General and his friend were returning to their hotel, the former said, "I am afraid, Doctor, you were too explicit about the jugular artery, for I observed Castlereagh to be in a strange mood when you finished your anatomical lecture." It is needless to state that many years did not elapse before Lord C. committed suicide by cutting his throat with a penknife.

Dr Howell related this incident to me at Brighton in 1849.

LOUIS PHILIPPE AT TWICKENHAM.—Early in this century Louis Philippe lived with his brothers in a small cottage at Twickenham, where, though fond of conviviality, he practised the most rigid economy. They had only one man-servant and a maid-of-all-work. Towards the end of his chequered life he was heard to say in passing the cottage, "There I passed some of the happiest days of my life; but during that period I had to struggle against poverty, without receiving aid from any one." The three royal brothers had a tilbury, which they drove by turns ; but they gave both man and horse a holiday on Sundays.

I received this little anecdote from a friend who when young resided at Richmond, and was intimately acquainted with the fallen monarch. Louis Philippe resided in England till 1808, when he embarked for Malta, carrying thither, for change of climate, his surviving brother, the Count Beaujolais, then in a rapid consumption. The Count's health was such that it was found necessary to stop at Gibraltar, where H. R. H. died. Louis Philippe afterwards proceeded to Sicily to return thanks for various favours he had received from the King of Naples, and there he met his future wife in the king's second daughter, the Princess Amélie. There can be little question but that it was a love match, as at that period there did not appear to be the remotest chance of Louis Philippe succeeding to his patrimonial estates, much less to the crown of France; and it was by many considered a foolish marriage. There were many difficulties in the way of their being married; but these were, however, surmounted, and the royal pair were united on the 25th November 1809, at Naples.

After the downfall of Napoleon the First, Louis Philippe returned to Paris, contrary to the wishes of Louis XVIII., whose jealousy was sharpened by the wily Talleyrand. There he occupied himself with the culture of his vast estates, the education of his children, and the formation of a political party, which a few years later placed him on the throne of France.

ETON COLLEGE IN 1810.—When Dr Keate, the head master of the Lower School, was elevated to the Upper, he did not bring with him a popular name ; his abrupt, blunt, and somewhat rude manner, which contrasted strongly with the mild and polished bearing of his predecessor, Dr Goodall, did not tend to remove the unfavourable impression his antecedents had produced. The consequence was a good deal of disaffection, which showed itself in various ways. The most remarkable and successful trick which was played off on him, by some bold and skilful boy whose name to this day remains undisclosed, I will endeavour to describe. The head master, when he came from his private chambers to the upper schoolroom, had to pass through the old library by a private door, the key of which

Keate always carried in his pocket. One morning coming to his accustomed duties, on reaching the door he tried in vain to insert the key into the lock; the key could not be forced into it: and no wonder, for it was afterwards discovered that a small bullet had been dexterously inserted into the wards of the lock. The little autocrat, (for Keate was diminutive in stature,) thus compelled to sound a retreat, descended the private stairs, and after making a long detour under the colonnade, entered the upper schoolroom: he strode along full of ire and breathing vengeance; which, however, was never gratified. But the game was not yet played out; for when the Doctor got to the upper end of the school, and ascended the steps which led to the pulpit, he found the door which led into it was screwed up. Keate was considered to be a sort of pocket Hercules, but nevertheless all his efforts to force open the door proved ineffectual. Foiled here, he rushed to the other side; but the same result awaited him. The well-known Eton cry, "Boo, boo," was now reiterated from one end of the schoolroom to the other, which naturally added fuel to the flame of the Doctor's wrath. Plucky to the last, with one bound he vaulted over the doorway into his sanctum, his face glowing with rage like a fiery meteor. Off flew his three-corner cocked-hat, and down he sat ; but his seat being smeared all over with cobbler's wax, the little man found that he could not rise without an awkward rent in his silk breeches. I leave it to the reader's imagination to picture the result of this species of practical joking : it certainly did not improve the Doctor's temper, for he grew more unpopular with the school, and he avenged himself upon the persons of delinquent boys.

FLOGGING AT ETON, UNDER DR KEATE.—Eton under Dr Keate was conducted on a system of brutal severity, which never ought to have been permitted. I recollect that a row—or, as it was foolishly denominated, a rebellion—took place there in 1809, owing to the vexatious and tyrannical conduct of the head master, who had ordered an extra muster roll during the summer months, by which the boys were precluded from amusing themselves as before at cricket, boating, &c. On this occasion, no fewer than ninety grown-up boys were flogged for the crime of declining to comply with the irksome regulation. Though this affair occurred nearly sixty years ago, I really cannot think of it without indignation ; for I remember that the fear of the birch was so strong at the time that no boy went up with his lesson without trembling with apprehension of being put in the bill for a flogging.

Keate, however, paid the penalty for his excessive severity, for he never got on in the Church ; while the late excellent Archbishop Sumner, who was a tutor under Keate, and never got a boy flogged, owed his position to his kindness towards those who afterwards became public men.

GEORGE IV. WHEN PRINCE OF WALES.—When everybody took snuff, the Prince of Wales followed the fashion ; or rather led it, for he was known to possess the finest collection of snuff-boxes that were to be had for love or money. His Royal Highness . never permitted his friends or acquaintances the liberty to take a pinch out of his box, so that every one had his own particular *tabatière*. How different this was to times gone by, when a great man delighted in nothing so much as to offer any one he was acquainted with a pinch of snuff : for instance, the greatest dandy of the time to which I am referring, thought it an honour to take a *prise* from the poet Dryden's box; but there was unfortunately a wide difference between the Prince and the poet.

Mrs Fitzherbert, who was considered by many to be the wife of the Prince Regent, lived in a magnificent house in Tilney Street, Hyde Park, in great state, her carriages and servants being the same as those H. R. H. made use of. Brummel, who was then on good terms with the Prince, called on this lady one day accompanied by his friend Pierrepoint, and found the Prince seated on a sofa. The Prince, according to the Beau's statement, appeared sullen and evidently annoyed at the visit of the two gentlemen, and on Brummel's taking a pinch of snuff and carelessly placing his box on a small table nearly opposite H. R. H., the Prince observed, " Mr Brummel, the place for your box is in your pocket, and not on the table." Another specimen of H. R. H.'s rudeness may be cited. Lord Barrymore called at Carlton House one day, and was ushered into the Prince's private room; on entering he placed his hat on a chair, when H. R. H. observed, in a sarcastic manner, " My Lord, a well-bred man places his hat under his arm on entering a room, and on his head when out of doors."

BEAU BRUMMEL'S AUNT, MRS SEARLE.—At the
small entrance of the Green Park, opposite Clarges
Street, and close to the reservoir, there stood some
years back a neat cottage surrounded by a court-
yard, with stables for cows. The exterior of the
cottage betokened no small degree of comfort and
modest affluence; nor did the interior disappoint
those who formed that opinion. Its inmates were
two old ladies, dressed in the style of Louis XV.,
with high, lace caps and dresses of brocaded silk.

In the autumn of 1814 I happened to stroll into
the Park to see these cows, which were famed for
their colour and symmetry. It was the hour for
milking them, and one of the old ladies, observing
my curiosity to see that operation performed, came
up to the palings and begged me to walk in. I
readily complied, and remained some time, then,
thanking her for the honour she had done me, I took
my leave, having accepted her invitation to pay her
a visit the next evening; which I did. After sa-
luting Mrs Searle and inquiring after her health, I led
her on to talk on divers matters. She had an excellent memory, was replete with *esprit*, and appeared
to possess a knowledge of everything and everybody.
I soon discovered that the old lady was proud of her

blood, and she told me that she was aunt to George
Brummel, the Beau; that George III. had placed her
as gate-keeper of the Green Park, and that the Princess Mary had kindly furnished her little cottage.
Her description of the Royal Family was somewhat
interesting. She said, that one day the Prince of
Wales, accompanied by the beautiful Marchioness
of Salisbury, called upon her, and as it was a beautiful summer's evening, stopped to see her cows milked.
Her nephew George Brummel, who had only a day
or two before left Eton, happened to be present.
The Prince, attracted by his nice manners, entered
into conversation with him, and before he left said,
" As I find you intend to be a soldier, I will give
you a commission in my own regiment." Tears of
gratitude filled the youth's eyes, and he fell on his
knees and kissed the royal hand. Shortly after,
George Brummel's commission in the 10th Hussars
was made out, and he was soon quartered with his
regiment at Brighton. Mrs Searle added, "But what is
most singular, a striking change took place in my
nephew's behaviour ; for so soon as he began to mix
in society with the Prince, his visits to me became
less and less frequent, and now he hardly ever calls
to see his old aunt."

ONE WAY OUT OF A DILEMMA.—I recollect when a boy seeing a strange couple, a Mr and Mrs Turbeville, who were famed for their eccentricities. Mr Turbeville was related to Sir Thomas Picton, but did not possess the talent or discretion of the gallant General. Upon one occasion, at a dinner at Dunraven Castle, after the ladies had retired, Mr Turbeville observed to a gentleman present, that the woman who had sat at his right was the ugliest he had ever seen; upon which the gentleman said, " I am sorry to hear that you think my wife so ill-looking." " Oh, no, sir, I have made a mistake ; I meant the lady who sat on my left." " Well, sir, she is my sister." " It can't be helped, sir, then ; for if what you have said is true, I must confess I never saw such an ugly family during the course of my life."

ANECDOTE OF A LORD-LIEUTENANT OF IRELAND.— In times gone by, when Lords-Lieutenants thought more of love and beauty than the land they were sent to govern, and considered they had a right to monopolise every pretty girl who appeared at the Castle balls, two sisters, the beautiful Misses Gunn, were the objects of the Viceroy's assiduous attention. Of course, they were much envied both by mothers and daughters for the attention shown them by the Viceroy and his family. All went on swimmingly until one day a young lady, only about sixteen years of age, and of surpassing beauty, a Miss Woodcock, made her appearance at one of the drawing-rooms. She came as if from the waves of the Channel, for nobody knew her name or family, and she was known by the cognomen of the beautiful Venus. The Lord-Lieutenant at once discarded the Misses Gunn, and lavished jewellery and presents upon the youthful Venus in so barefaced a manner, that society began to be alarmed, and gave the new beauty the cold shoulder. Bunbury, the celebrated caricaturist, happening to be at Dublin, turned the scandal to good account, by drawing a capital likeness of the Viceroy, dressed as Robinson Crusoe, carrying a *Gun* upon each shoulder, and a *Woodcock* at his left side ; denoting that his affections lay in that quarter.

MR LAWRENCE, THE CELEBRATED SURGEON.—It was my good fortune to have known Mr Lawrence, who was allowed to have been the most scientific, as well as one of the most skilful surgeons England or Europe could boast of at that time. The opinion entertained of him by the faculty was evinced by

the many high encomiums passed upon his talents by
his contemporaries.   He was the most accomplished
and gentlest of mankind, and ever ready to render the
slightest service to a friend in distress.   Upon one
occasion I called upon him at his house in White-
hall, opposite the Admiralty, and told him that
half an hour before I had seen a pretty girl, an
opera dancer, unable to move from her sofa owing
to "soft corns," which precluded her from appearing on the stage.   "Bring her here, my friend
Gronow, and I will endeavour to cure her; but do
not mention to any one that I have turned chiro-
podist."   I lost no time in calling upon the
danseuse, and prevailed upon her to place herself
under the care of my skilful friend.   Some few
days elapsed, when I met Lawrence in his carriage
and was invited by him to take a drive, during
which he asked me if I had seen the young lady,
whom he had operated upon and completely cured.
Upon my replying in the negative, he said, "It is
always so when you render a service to persons
possessing neither principle nor feeling; you are
sure to be treated with ingratitude."   This lady
became immensely rich, and I regret to add that

the surgeon's fee was never paid, which I had good reason to know amounted to twenty guineas.

ESCAPADE OF AN OFFICER OF THE 3D FOOT GUARDS.—It is nearly fifty years since a young officer in the 3d Guards, smitten with the charms of Lady Betty Charteris, who was remarkable for her beauty and attainments, determined at all hazards to carry her off and marry her. Her father put a stop to any legitimate, straightforward wooing, by forbidding her to encourage the attentions of the young officer, who was too poor to maintain her in the position in which she had been brought up. When the London season was over, the family left for Scotland, and my friend, Andrew C——, decided on following his lady-love. Andrew was young, handsome, romantic, and sentimental; but a brave fellow, and had fought gallantly at Waterloo. After consulting several of his intimate friends, who recommended perseverance, he determined to further his scheme by disguising himself. So, with the aid of a black wig and a suit of seedy clothes, he engaged the services of an Italian organ-grinder, and took his place beside him on one of the Edinburgh coaches.

In the course of a few days the pair arrived at a village close to the mansion of the lady's father, and a correspondence was carried on between the lovers. They met, and after a great many urgent entreaties on the part of the enamoured swain, a day was arranged for the elopement. Andrew next gained over the head gardener, by stating that he had just arrived from Holland, and was up to the latest dodges in tulip-growing ; then a mania in England. By this means he contrived to be constantly on the premises, and to obtain frequent interviews with the charming Lady Betty. The day fixed at length arrived, and the organ-grinder (then a rarity in Scotland) was introduced on the scene ; his sprightly airs fascinated the servants, who thronged to listen to him, and meanwhile a postchaise and four was driven up, out of sight of the house, according to a previous understanding between the lovers, who were ready for instant flight. Unluckily there was an excessively vigilant governess in attendance on Lady Betty, and at the moment when affairs seemed most prosperous, this duenna was at her post at the young lady's side in the garden. Andrew, feeling that everything depended on some decisive action, suddenly appeared, and ejaculating, "Now or never!" caught hold of his dulcinea's arm, and attempted to hurry in the direction of the chaise. The dragon interposed, and clung to the young lady, screaming for assistance; her cries brought out the servants, the enraged father, and the inmates of the house to her assistance, and poor Andrew and the organ-man with his monkey were ejected from the premises. The young Guardsman, however, soon got over the sorrow caused by the failure of his scheme; but the nickname of "Merry Andrew," bestowed on him by his brother officers, stuck to him afterwards.

THE GOOD FORTUNE OF A PRETTY WOMAN.— More than half a century ago a lady, conspicuous in the aristocratic world, on returning from a courtly *fête* and arriving at her mansion about four o'clock in the morning, was informed by her servants that a female child had been left at the door, wrapped up in a blanket. She desired that the infant might be taken care of; and, in the course of time, the child became a servant in the establishment. The girl grew to be a remarkable specimen of female beauty; her form was exquisitely

E

modelled ; her complexion was delicate and bloom-
ing ; her features were regular, and she was remarkable for her large blue, thoughtful eyes.   But
her greatest charm consisted in a most engaging
and lovable smile.   It was difficult to gaze upon
that face without feeling an interest in Clotilde far
beyond that which generally accompanies the con-
templation of ordinary beauty.   Although educated
in the servants' hall, yet, by that singular instinct
which some women possess, she had learned to make
her conversation and manner acceptable and engaging to educated persons, whether male or female.
The titled lady whom she knew as her protector
made her her confidential maid, and Clotilde soon
became the companion of her mistress.

She was not more than eighteen years of age
when an Admiral of the British navy, who visited
the house, fell desperately in love with her.   It was
during the period of the great wars of Napoleon the
First, and the Admiral, being employed in cruising
about the Mediterranean, was absent from London
for long periods ; but he never failed to correspond
with Clotilde, and his letters were regularly placed
before her mistress.   The girl used to turn into
ridicule the passionate language of the old sailor ;

but time passed on. and the Admiral returned, having distinguished himself, and become known as the intimate friend of the immortal Nelson ; and, within six months afterwards, Clotilde became the wife of one of the most distinguished officers of the British navy.

As frequently occurs when a young and beautiful woman of humble extraction is allied to a man in advanced years, and finds herself surrounded by men occupying the highest position in society, Clotilde became susceptible to attentions which were paid with a view to undermine her virtue. Amongst her admirers was a royal Duke, who afterwards ascended the throne of Great Britain ; and there is every reason to believe that many public acts of the navy and army originated in her influence. In short, the marriage was anything but a happy one, although the lady had daughters who were married to rich and noble foreigners. In the course of time the Admiral ignored her amours ; and it was well known in London society that my lady had her friends, and the Admiral his.

As Clotilde advanced in life, she fascinated and formed an intimacy with one of the most wealthy of British peers. By pandering to the eccentricities of the noble Lord, her authority over him became absolute. It was through this nobleman that she bestowed magnificent doweries on her daughters, and became possessed of a colossal fortune. Although her conduct was notoriously immoral, she was countenanced and visited by persons who, as is too frequently the case, permit their morality to become exceedingly elastic in the presence of wealth. Later in life, she thought it advisable to remove to Naples, where accident threw her in the way of a French lady's-maid, who in course of time obtained an alarming influence over his Lordship. Ever adroit, and possessing, intuitive perception and forethought, the lady made friends with the Frenchwoman; and when his Lordship's will was opened, it revealed an engagement which the rival ladies had previously concocted: Lady S—— became the legatee to an immense fortune, whilst her maid was moderately provided for.

Her great aim, after the death of the nobleman in question, was to become a respectable member of society. She invited people to magnificent dinners, became very devout, gave away a great deal of money in charity, and indeed did everything that such women do under similar circumstances. Her career is another illustration of what a pretty and clever woman, without heart or conscience, can accomplish, if smiled upon by fortune.

COLONEL, OR "BULL," TOWNSHEND.—When the Grenadier Guards returned to London from Cambrai, where they had been quartered some considerable time, the first thing that was proposed by the officers, was to invite their colonel, the Duke of York, to a banquet at the Thatched House, St James's Street. His Royal Highness, in a letter full of feeling and good taste, in which he alluded to the gallantry of the regiment he commanded, accepted the invitation, and, as was the custom upon such occasions, the army agents of the regiment were also invited. After dinner, Colonel Townshend commonly called the Bull, addressed the Duke, stating that, as he was then in command of the old battalion, he hoped H. R. H. would permit him to propose a toast. The Duke bowed assent, when the Bull bellowed out, "I propose the health of Mr Greenwood, to whom we are all of us so much indebted." This toast was ill chosen, for the Duke of York owed his army agents at that moment nearly fifty thousand pounds; but Townshend considered it a good joke, for he used frequently to boast of having astonished the Duke with his witty toast.   Townshend was the brother of Lord Sidney. He was considered by the officers and men of the regiment to be intrepid and brave.   He was unfortunately a slave to good cookery, which was the principal cause of his death.   Townshend, despite his imperfections, was generous and full of compassion to the soldiers he commanded; he stooped to no flattery, disdained all disloyal arts, and, in a word, was replete with sterling and splendid qualities.

Many of my old comrades can remember the excellent dinners Townshend used to give his friends at Cambrai.   I can call to mind that at one of those banquets, a young officer wilfully placed some ipecacuanha in one of Townshend's favourite *entrées*, of which he ate rather voraciously.   The consequence was, the Colonel was obliged to quit the dinner-table sooner than the rest of the *convives*. In the hurry of the moment he sat down upon a brittle vase, which broke, and caused a wound so severe that he was confined to his room for many weeks, and the doctor of the regiment was apprehensive of mortification, for it baffled for a considerable time his skill in effecting a cure ; but, fortunately, the gallant colonel recovered.

This unlucky accident became the subject of general conversation all over London, and the Duke of York happened at one of his dinners to allude to the awkward wound inflicted upon " the Bull," when Alvanley, who was dining at the royal table, observed in his off-hand manner, it was a *"filet de bœuf sauté."*

THE MARQUIS D'ALIGRE AND THE DENTIST.—In my third volume I alluded to the Marquis d'Aligre, who, though enormously rich, was known as the miser. When in England, during the war with France, he lived in great penury ; and his costume and appearance, half military and half Moravian, aided his assumption of the character of an impoverished *émigré*. Having lost nearly all his teeth, he determined to have a set of false ones, and accordingly called on Mr Spence, a celebrated dentist, who lived in Arlington Street, Piccadilly, to whom he represented himself as an *émigré* in urgent need of a set of teeth, but without means to pay for them. Mr Spence, commiserating the *poor* Frenchman, said he would make him a present of them : a day was fixed for their completion, and

D'Aligre joyfully promised to keep the appointment.

It happened that a countryman of D'Aligre's overheard the interview, and seeing Mr Spence in a thinking attitude, after the cunning old miser had left, said, "I suppose you are wondering why that old gentleman should be so ill-dressed, instead of being clothed like the generality of his countrymen." Mr Spence, not understanding the drift of the remark, begged he would be more explicit; upon which the gentleman repeated his remark, adding, "his penurious habits make us blush for our country." "What do you mean, sir?" reiterated the dentist. "I have promised to supply him with a new set of teeth *gratis,* for he represents himself as a poor nobleman without means; and unless you can prove that all he has said is false, I shall keep my word; on the other hand if I find that I have been imposed upon, I will make him repent it." The Frenchman said no more, but bowed and left. It happened, however, that among the many foreigners who participated in Mr Spence's hospitality, was the Duc de Bourbon, who, although very proud, was glad enough to dine with the dentist when invited; and at table one day, about this time, D'Aligre's name was mentioned. Mr Spence, anxious to learn more about the man, asked His Royal Highness if he could enlighten him on that point. The Duke said, " D'Aligre's wealth is unbounded ; he possesses more than all the *émigrés* from France."

Mr Spence's wrath and indignation on discovering the imposition were great ; and he determined to revenge himself. On the day appointed for the teeth to be ready, the Marquis made his appearance, and wished the dentist good morning in a most obsequious manner. Mr Spence took out of his pocket a piece of paper upon which was written, " The Marquis d'Aligre to Mr Spence for a set of false teeth, £200," at the same time holding in his other hand the coveted articles. D'Aligre again attempted to enact the " poor man ; " but the dentist gave him till the following day to pay for them. The money not being forthcoming, Mr Spence, in the presence of several persons, broke in pieces the false teeth he had made, saying, " Rather than be cheated and robbed in such a manner, I would discontinue my profession. But this affair will only hurt the Marquis ; for he will have to live upon slops until he finds some dentist whom he can defraud."

THE FRENCH ÉMIGRÉS.—We must all acknowledge that the self-denial and patience exhibited by the refugees from France at the time of the Revolution was worthy of the highest praise : nearly all the nobles and proprietors of that country quitted it during that fatal period, and the greater part came to England. Among them I recollect the Counts Forbin d'Offède, Choiseul, la Rochejacquelin, de Marin, and d'Aubenton, who gave lessons in French or music ; while the nobles De la Rochefoucauld, De Sainte-Aldégonde, and others, became linen merchants ; others, with equally great names, kept furnished lodgings, or *cafés;* while youths extremely well born and educated were obliged to seek situations as clerks in mercantile houses. One of the most remarkable men alive was obliged to emigrate to London—I mean Auber, the great composer. He became clerk in a bank, where he remained some years : it was the same establishment where the rich Greffulhe laid the foundation of a fortune which, it is said, exceeds at the present moment six millions sterling.

I have already mentioned the Marquis d'Aligre's conduct with regard to tradespeople ; and towards his own countrymen he was equally mean in refusing

them any assistance, although then in the enjoyment
of a princely income. After the affair with the dentist, London becoming too warm for him, he took his
departure for Germany with his wife, whose death
occurred there. It is the custom in that country on
such occasions, for an official to call at every house
proclaiming in a loud voice the age and titles of the
deceased, and the day fixed for the funeral; the
Marquis, desirous of avoiding expense, and being in
a measure compelled to respect the rule, employed
his servant to announce these particulars. Accordingly, the flunkey, dressed in a sorry threadbare suit
of black, carried out his master's orders by knocking
at every door, and exclaiming in a loud voice, "*Hier,
à six heures du soir, Madame la Marquise d'Aligre*
caput." As "caput" in the German language means
destroyed and broken to pieces, this announcement
rather astonished the natives.

The avarice of the Marquis so disgusted the inhabitants of Carlsbad that they determined by hook or
by crook to get rid of him. Every sort of practical
joke was played on him, and he at last quitted the
town just as a concert of rough music, or, in other
words, a *charivari*, which had been preparing for
some time, was about to be given in his *honour*.

THE EMPEROR ALEXANDER.—The Emperor Alexander was considered one of the politest men of his age. When attending the Congress at Aix la Chapelle, he would, out of compliment, put on the Prussian uniform when he visited the King of Prussia, the Austrian when he visited the Emperor of Austria, and the English uniform, in honour of our country, which was represented by the Duke of Wellington.

It is known that, prior to the disastrous Russian campaign, his majesty was an enthusiastic admirer of Napoleon, and it is said that when, according to custom, orders were exchanged between the sovereigns of Russia and France, the Emperor Alexander was so proud of the grand cross of the Legion of Honour, that, not content with wearing it in his button-hole, he had another cross made which, on grand occasions, was hung round the neck of his favourite horse. When Napoleon heard of this eccentricity he said, "My brother the Emperor can do what he likes at St Petersburg ; but if he adopted that plan in Paris, my Minister of Police would feel it his duty to consign him to Bicêtre (the madhouse) to prevent his being mobbed and laughed at by the public."

An Incident at the Battle of Borodino.— At the bloody battle of Borodino, the news of the great redoubt having been taken was carried to the Emperor Napoleon by a staff officer. The Emperor inquired whether the bearer of the message had been sent by General Caulaincourt, and the officer had begun his reply thus, "No, your majesty; I saw the General receive his death wound on entering the battery"—when he himself received a terrible wound, and fell from his horse insensible through loss of blood. The Emperor took off the cross of honour which he wore, and directed his aide-de-camp to place it on the poor fellow's breast. The wound was so severe that all the surgeons could do to resuscitate him proved for some time of no avail ; but happily, on one of the grenadiers slapping his hands, he opened his eyes and beheld the cross of the Legion of Honour with which he had been decorated by order of his sovereign, and was told that if he survived he would be promoted. Fortunately, youth and health carried him through, and the promise made to him was kept.

General Jacqueminot.—In 1814, soon after the

return of the Bourbons, General Jacqueminot and three other officers of the Bonaparte school dressed themselves like *émigrés*, went to the *café* Hardy, asked for the carte, and looking it over observed an *entrée* called "*Poulet à la Marengo*," upon which Jacqueminot observed, "No, that won't do ; it smells too much of the Revolution." A gentleman, sitting at the next table, who had served under the Emperor at the battle of Marengo, jumped up and exclaimed, "What the devil do those *émigrés* know of our battles ? They ran away from France when there was danger, but come back when it is over." Jacqueminot pretended to be very irate ; but going up to the gentleman in question said, in a low voice, "You are one of the right sort. I admire both your courage and frankness ; and if all men of our party would follow your example, there would not be a Bourbon left in Paris twenty-four hours longer."

Unfortunately for the young men who had acted the part of *émigrés*, it happened that one of the waiters was a policeman in disguise. He denounced them to the Government, who ordered the whole of them to appear before a court-martial ; they were tried, and condemned to lose their rank and pay in the army. Jacqueminot was so enraged with the police spy, that he caught hold of the man in the presence of the court, and would have murdered him, had not the President, who had formerly known Jacqueminot in Russia, cried aloud, " You are too brave to hurt that villain. All hail, Jacqueminot, as a hero!" Suddenly Jacqueminot recollected that the President had been saved by him at the battle of Borodino.

THE EMPEROR'S FUR CLOAK. — When Napoleon I. assumed the title of Emperor, he received from the Emperor of Russia a magnificent fur cloak, which, it was reported, cost a fabulous sum. The Princess Pauline, being desirous of possessing this costly mantle, by exercising her bewitching fascinations, prevailed upon her imperial brother to give it her. It was generally believed that she had given her affections to a young officer, who was considered very handsome ; but he, not content with being thus favoured, was very jealous of her, and objected to her wearing the mantle, as she thereby attracted great attention : the Princess, therefore, made him a present of it.

This gentleman, a M. de Canouville, vain of his good looks, which the superb cloak set off to advantage, determined on wearing it at a grand review of the Guards, prior to their departure for Russia. He was riding a very young horse, which had not been sufficiently broken, and when the Emperor arrived on the ground with his escort, the sudden burst of music and the firing of cannon so frightened the animal that he bolted at railroad speed across the review ground. Unluckily for the coxcomb, this *contretemps* did not escape the keen eye of the Emperor, who recognised the imperial gift ; and, on his return to the Tuileries, he gave orders to send the culprit to join the army, saying that the fur cloak would keep him warm amid the snows and ice of Russia, from whence it came.

A MARRIAGE QUICKLY ARRANGED.—When the expedition was about to sail from France for St Domingo, the First Consul named his brother-in-law, General Leclerc, commander-in-chief of the invading army. The General went, as is usual in such cases, to make his bow to his superior, prior to his departure. Bonaparte addressed him in rather a laconic tone, saying, "You must quit Paris to-morrow evening." "But, sire, it is impossible," replied General Leclerc. "Nothing is impossible :

my orders must be obeyed. I have no objection to your taking my sister Pauline, your wife, with you ; but go you must." "But, sire, *my* sister will be left behind in France, without money or friends." "Oh! is that all ?" replied the First Consul. "I will send her a husband to-morrow, with rank and money. Begone, sir, and come back in the course of to-morrow, and all will be arranged to your satisfaction." General Leclerc left, muttering, "*Nous ne devons plus qu'obéir. Nous avons trouvé un maître là où nous ne voulions qu'un protecteur.*"

Meanwhile General Davoust entered the First Consul's cabinet, when Bonaparte said to him, "I am glad you are come, for I have found you a wife, young and accomplished." "But, sire, I am engaged to a young lady, and have promised to marry her as soon as I have procured your consent." "Not a word more, Davoust, about your promise ; but come here to-morrow morning, and you shall know more about your future wife." It was no use to kick against the pricks, so Davoust arrived at the palace the next morning, where he met Leclerc ; neither being aware of the relation in which they were about to stand to each other. They sent in their names ; and Bonaparte calling them in, told Leclerc

F

to accompany Davoust to St Germain, where he was to introduce the latter to his sister. Madame de Campan, in her position of directress of the convent, was to accompany them back to Paris with the young lady in question, and all were to present themselves at the Tuileries at a given hour. There the marriage-contract was signed. Napoleon settled a large dowery on the bride, and agreed to provide her with everything necessary for her *corbeille de mariage.* Thus, in twenty-four hours, one General found a brother-in-law in a rival, the other a brother-in-law in an engaged lover, and the young lady a husband in the man who was justly called " the bloody Davoust."

Napoleon the First's Love of Music. — The Emperor Napoleon I. was passionately fond of Italian music, and wherever the Court stayed, several of the best *artistes* of the day might be found, who were treated with the greatest consideration. Paesiello was the Emperor's favourite amongst them ; indeed, he took an unbounded interest in his success, and was so enchanted one day by a song Paesiello had just written, that he caught him by the hand, saying, " Without doubt

you are the greatest composer that ever lived."
"No, sire, I am not," replied he ; "while Cimarosa
lives, to him must be given the palm."

Paesiello wrote the opera of "Proserpine," which
was brought out at Paris under the auspices of the
Emperor ; but somehow or other it did not suit the
French taste, and proved a failure. Napoleon was
furious at the non-success of his *protégé's* opera, and
observed, "It is not to be wondered at, for the French
understand nothing of music." Paesiello thought so
too ; for though so highly patronised by the Emperor
and court, he quitted France in disgust. It was
with difficulty that a man of musical genius could
be found to replace the Italian in the Emperor's
favour; but Méhul was at last thought of, and
summoned to the Tuileries. When he was informed of Napoleon's wishes, the composer solicited
an interview with the great man, and after the usual
salutation, informed the Emperor that he could not
accept the proffered honour unless allowed to
divide the perquisites with his friend Cherubini.
This was refused ; Napoleon saying, "I can never
permit that, for I hate the man." "It is a pity,
sire, that you do not like him, for he is my superior
in every way." "I care not for that. I still per-

sist in refusing to have that man near me, and
nothing can change my determination." "Then,"
replied Méhul, "I am compelled to decline the
flattering offer your majesty has made me."

The reason why the Emperor was so inimical to
Cherubini was that, when Napoleon returned from
the Italian campaign with only the rank of General,
he on one occasion offered a remark not very flattering to the composer ; and Cherubini retorted,
"Mêlez vous, Général, de gagner des batailles ; c'est
votre métier.   Laissez-moi faire le mien, auquel
vous n'entendez rien."   For this Cherubini was
never pardoned.   Méhul, though he had refused the
Emperor's offer, still remained in favour at Court,
and his pieces were criticised by the Emperor ; who
often told Méhul that his compositions were too
German, and not to be compared with those of the
Italian school.   "The Germans, in composing, think
too much of science, but are unmindful of that
which touches the heart.   This fault is also shared
by the French composers : all their operas want
grace and gaiety."   On the appearance of the opera
"L'Irato" which is written in the Italian style, Napoleon, ignorant as to who the composer was, begged

Méhul to be present. After some demur he' consented. The overture was much applauded, and
the Emperor observed to Méhul, "Now, you see,
there is nothing like Italian music." The opera
then proceeded, and was throughout much admired
by the audience ; and when at the end the authors
of the piece were called before the curtain, Méhul,
the composer, and Marsollier, the writer of the
piece, appeared, and were received with boisterous
applause. The Emperor, delighted, sent for Méhul,
and cried out, in a tone loud enough to be heard by
many present, "*Attrapez moi toujours de même,
mon cher Méhul, et je m'en rejouirai pour votre
gloire et mes plaisirs.*"

PARTING OF NAPOLEON AND MADAME MÈRE.—
Talma was present at the last parting at the Malmaison between the Emperor and his mother, and he
said that it was one of the most tragic scenes he
had ever witnessed. When the last moment arrived,
the Empress-mother, prostrated with grief, and
with tears streaming from her eyes, could only
utter, in a tremulous voice, "*Adieu, mon fils!
adieu !*" And Napoleon was so affected, that he

caught hold of both her hands, cried, "*Adieu, ma mère!*" and burst into tears as he left her.   The mother was destined never again to meet the son

> " Whose filial piety excels
> Whatever Grecian story tells."

PRINCE EUGÈNE BEAUHARNAIS.—Soon after the fall of Napoleon, the Emperor of Russia, together with the other allied sovereigns, desirous of showing their respect and admiration for the conduct of Prince Eugène, offered him the Duchy of Genoa. The following was the reply sent by the Viceroy to the one he had received making the offer :—

" SIRE,—I have received your Majesty's propositions.   They certainly are very flattering, but they will in no way change my determination.   Neither the duchy nor the kingdom of Italy will induce me to become a traitor ; and rather than follow the example of Murat, I would prefer entering the ranks again as a private soldier.

" You state that the Emperor Napoleon was not kind to me.   I have forgotten all this.   I know, however, that I owe everything to him—my fortune, my rank and titles.   If he should require my services again, I would serve him with all my ability ; for my body belongs to him, as does my heart.

" I flatter myself that in refusing to agree to the offer you have done me the honour to make, your Majesty will appreciate my conduct, and assure me the continuance of your esteem.

" EUGÈNE BEAUHARNAIS."

THE PRESENT EMPEROR OF THE FRENCH WHEN A BOY.—Prince Louis Napoleon, when at the age of six, lived with his mother, Queen Hortense, at the Malmaison, with whom resided the Empress Josephine ; who, it will be remembered, received the allied sovereigns there in 1814, after Napoleon I. was exiled to Elba. The Emperor of Russia when in Paris scarcely passed a day without visiting those exalted ladies, and on each occasion he breakfasted or dined with them. The Queen told her children, that when the Emperor Alexander called, every mark of attention and respect was to be paid to his Imperial Majesty ; for to him, and him alone, they owed everything they possessed in the world. Prince Louis listened to his mother's precepts with great attention, but said nothing. The next time the Czar came, however, the little fellow sidled up to him and quietly placed on one of the Czar's fingers a ring, which his uncle Prince Eugène, the Viceroy of Italy, had given him. The boy, on being asked by his mother what he meant, said, " I have only this ring, which my uncle gave me ; but I have given it to the Emperor Alexander, because he has been so kind to you, dear mamma." The autocrat smiled, and placing the gift on his watch-chain, said he would never part with it, but would keep it in remembrance of the noble trait of generosity shown by one so young. The Queen replied, " Sire, my son Louis keeps nothing for himself : the other day I gave him some pretty buttons, but he gave them away to some of his play-mates ; and when I reproached him for so doing, his answer was, " *Vous voulez, maman, me procurer un plaisir en me les offrant, et vous m'en procurez deux ; celui de recevoir de vous, maman, un jolie chose, et ensuite le plaisir de la donner à un autre.*"

Another anecdote, showing the good nature of Louis Napoleon, was related to me by the late M. Mocquard, with whom I was well acquainted. After leaving the Malmaison, Queen Hortense settled by the Lake of Constance, where the young Prince was constantly in the habit of relieving poor people by giving away his pocket-money. One day he observed a family in the greatest distress, but having no money to give them ; he took off his coat and boots and gave them to these poor people, saying that he was sorry that he had not any money for them, as he had given away the allowance his mother made him to some other poor persons who had just passed by the house ; but he hoped they would dispose of his clothes to relieve their wants. The weather at this time was very cold, and the ground covered with snow ; the Prince nevertheless, trudged through it towards home, and when near the house was met by Mocquard, who expressed his surprise at seeing him in that state. The little fellow, then ten years old, replied, " I have given away my clothes to some poor people to prevent them from starving." Mocquard added, that " the Emperor is never so happy as when he can relieve the distressed."

JEROME BONAPARTE AND CARDINAL FESCH.— Jerome, the youngest brother of the great Emperor, was when young extremely wild and extravagant. He was always in debt, and would borrow money of any one who would trust him. Upon one occasion he called upon his uncle, the Car-

dinal Fesch, who invited him to dinner.   The Cardinal was a great amateur of paintings, and his
gallery contained some of the finest specimens of
the old masters.   After dinner, the Cardinal was
on the point of quitting the dining-room, when
Jerome followed him, and asked for the loan of 500
francs.   The old Cardinal refused to lend him the
money, whereupon Jerome became furious, drew his
sword, swore vengeance against his uncle, and
began cutting at everything about him.   Unfortunately his sword fell upon a *chef-d'œuvre* by Van-
dyke, which the Cardinal, upon his return to the
dining-room, observing, called out in a loud voice,
" Stop, young man ! sheathe your sword, and here
are your 500 francs ! "

THE CZAR AND THE APPLE GIRL.—In the neighbourhood of the Tuileries there used to be a small
fair, where apples, toys, cakes, &c., were sold. When
the Emperor Alexander was in Paris, he one day
strolled through it, and remarking a very pretty
fascinating girl staring intently at him from one of
the stalls, he asked her the reason.   " I am looking
at you, sir," she replied, " because you are the very
counterpart of the Emperor of Russia ; but you can-

not be that great personage, or you would not lower yourself by talking to a poor apple girl." The autocrat replied, "Whether I am the Emperor or not, rest assured, my dear, that were I to stay much longer in your company I should lose my heart; but, however," continued he, presenting her with a louis d'or, " can you tell me the address of the Emperor of Russia, for I am anxious to find it out?" She gave up her stall to one of her friends, and volunteered to accompany the great man to find himself. On their arrival at the hotel, he begged she would walk in. "No, sir: I have shown you where the Emperor lives, which I think is all that you require; so good morning, sir." "No, no, that is not all, my little angel; you must now tell me where you live." "Well, sir, I am to be found at my stall." The result of this was, that the girl found her way to St Petersburg, where she lived for some time under the Emperor's protection: she afterwards married a great nobleman, and became the mother of the man who played the most prominent part in the Crimean war.

DE SOUZA, THE PORTUGUESE AMBASSADOR.—The fame of De Souza for the piquancy of his wit and his readiness in retort was general at every court in Europe.   When in England, he had the *entrée* of Carlton House, and was on terms of intimacy with the Prince Regent.   At that time his Royal Highness's life was spent in great dissipation, and those at court followed his example.   A hundredth part of what actually occurred at Carlton House would afford rare materials for anecdote ; though it is only right to add that much of the scandal propagated respecting this period was pure invention.

De Souza, though perhaps the ugliest little man I ever saw, was nevertheless remarkable for the charm and grace of his conversation ; and there was no one then in the diplomatic world, Tallyrand excepted, who attained greater perfection in what is called the *art de vivre* than the Portuguese ambassador.   Our hero revelled in the gossip and scandal of society, and he used to amuse the Prince Regent with frequent anecdotes and witty sayings from both Lisbon and the Brazils.   His sayings made everybody laugh, and his droll manner was inimitable.   He had a mania for relating stories about women, which sometimes made even the Regent blush.   At dinner at Carlton House one day he observed that some men were addicted to extraordinary tastes, and commenced a story in illustration, when the Prince exclaimed, "Halt! no more at present, De Souza. You shall tell us the rest when the cloth is removed." After the servants had retired, the Prince said, "Now, De Souza, continue the story which you began during dinner." "Well, your Royal Highness, my story will not occupy much time; it is merely that a friend of mine in Lisbon was exceedingly fond of peacock's tails." "Well, what then?" "Ah! your Royal Highness, he preferred those ornaments to the most beautiful women: indeed, he was so infatuated with them, that he sometimes fancied himself a peacock." "Come, come, De Souza, this is too much: we cannot swallow such nonsense." "Well, sire, I can only vouch for what I saw, and that was, a nun rubbing down the tails upon my friend's back, and saying, What a beautiful bird you are!"

LORD HAY AND THE PRINCE REGENT.—At the Prince Regent's first levee, in 1815, Lord Hay, eldest son of the Earl of Errol, was presented with other officers of the Guards to have the honour of kissing hands; when the Prince gave his hand to be kissed, the young nobleman, unversed in court etiquette, caught hold of it and shook it with all his might. The

Prince, though a very proud and formal personage, seeing the youth of the young soldier, took the salute in good part, and inquired how the Earl of Errol was. Lord James Murray, observing that something had occurred which was creating a laugh at the expense of his young countryman, good-naturedly took him by the arm and removed him from the royal presence. "What have you been doing, Lord Hay," inquired Lord James Murray, "to be the cause of so much mirth?" "I don't know, unless it was that I shook the Prince's hand with all my might." "Only that, my Lord!" replied Lord James; "why, you have committed a flagrant breach of etiquette." "How so?" inquired Lord Hay. "Why, you ought only to have placed the royal hand to your mouth, instead of shaking it." "Oh, my Lord, I will make amends. I will return and apologise to his Royal Highness." "No, no, Lord Hay; that will make matters worse." The same evening Lord James Murray dined with the Prince, and mentioned to his Royal Highness what Lord Hay proposed doing, by way of making amends for his *gaucherie.* The Prince was extremely amused, and observed, he never had seen so handsome a young soldier in the uniform of the Guards.

Lord Hay, a few days subsequently, left England for Brussels, to join his regiment, the 1st Foot Guards; and at the battle of Quatre Bras, whilst gallantly leading his company in a charge against the French sharp-shooters, this young nobleman received a musket ball in the heart, which, of course, caused instant death.

In those days the 1st Foot Guards were officered by some of the handsomest young men that England could boast of. I recollect with pride the names of several of them, viz. :—The two Foxes, William and Sackville; the two Bridgemans; Johnny Lyster, Augustus Dashwood, Cradock, Daniel Tighe, Douglas, Erskine of Mar, Alix, Thoroton, Lord Hay, Barrington, Langrishe, and many others whose names, alas! I now forget. But as nothing is perfect in this world, I must in justice state, that notwithstanding the noble list I have particularised, there were in the regiment one or two of the ugliest men, perhaps, that the world ever beheld.

THE PRINCE REGENT AND CARLTON HOUSE.— One of the meanest and most ugly edifices that ever disfigured London, notwithstanding it was screened by a row of columns, was Carlton House, the residence of the Prince Regent. It was condemned by everybody who possessed taste; and Canova the sculptor, on being asked his opinion of it, said, "There are at Rome a thousand buildings more beautiful, and whose architecture is in comparison faultless, any one of which would be more suitable for a princely residence than that ugly barn." This building was constantly under repair, but never improved, for no material alterations were made in its appearance. The first step towards improvement should have been to give it a coat of "lime-wash," for it was blackened with dust and soot. Apropos of the alterations: the workmen engaged therein were a great source of annoyance to the Prince, who, pretending that he did not like to be stared at, objected to their entering by the gate-. way. It is certain that the Prince Regent kept himself as much aloof as possible from the lower class of his subjects, and was annoyed by the natural curiosity of those who hold that as "a cat may look at a king," permission for that luxury should not be denied to bipeds.

I recollect that, having called, when on guard, upon Sir Benjamin Bloomfield about the sale of a cob, which he gave me to understand he wanted for the Prince Regent, while conversing we were interrupted by the entrance of the Prince, attended by M'Mahon and the eccentric "Tommy Tit." His Royal Highness was in an angry humour, and blurted out in his rage, "I will not allow those maid-servants to look at me when I go in and out; and if I find they do so again, I will have them discharged." I could hardly believe my ears, that a man born to the highest rank could take umbrage at such pardonable curiosity. But while riding in Hyde Park the next day, I was joined by General Baylie, who it seemed had been a spectator of this outburst of wrath: he told me that the Prince constantly complained of the servants staring at him, and that strict orders had been given to discharge any one caught repeating the offence.

LORD BARRYMORE.—This nobleman came of a very old family, and when of age succeeded to a fine estate. He acquired no small degree of notoriety from his love of pugilism and cock-fighting; but his *forte* lay in driving, and few coachmen on the northern road could "tool" a four-in-hand like him. His Lordship was one of the founders of the "Whip Club." The first time I ever saw Lord Barrymore was one fine evening while taking a stroll in Hyde Park. The weather was charming, and a great number of the *bon-ton* had assembled to witness the departure of the Four-in-Hand Club. Conspicuous among all the "turns-out" was that of his Lordship, who drove four splendid grays, unmatched in symmetry, action, and power. Lord Barrymore was, like Byron and Sir Walter Scott, club-footed. I discovered this defect the moment he got off his box to arrange something wrong in the harness. If there had been a competitive examination, the prize of which would be given to the most proficient in slang and vulgar phraseology, it would have been safe to back his Lordship as the winner against the most foul-mouthed of costermongers ; for the way he blackguarded his servants for the misadjustment of a strap was horrifying. On returning home, I dressed and went to the Club to dine, where I alluded to the choice morsels of English vernacular that had fallen from the noble whip's mouth in addressing his servants, and was assured that such was his usual language when out of temper.

In addition to his "drag" in the "Four-in-hand Club," Lord Barrymore sported a very pretty "Stanhope," in which he used to drive about town, accompanied by a little boy, whom the world denominated his tiger. It was reported that Lord Barrymore had, in his younger days, been taken much notice of by the Prince Regent ; in fact, he had been the boon companion of His Royal Highness, and had assisted at the orgies that used to take place at Carlton House, where he was a constant visitor. Notwithstanding this, Lord Barrymore was considered by those intimately acquainted with him to be a man of literary talents. He certainly was an accomplished musician, a patron of the drama, and a great friend of Cooke, Kean, and the two Kembles ; yet I have heard a host of crimes attributed to his Lordship. This, if not a libel, showed that the connexion existing between the Prince Regent and this nobleman could not have been productive of good results, and tends to confirm the impression that the profligate life led by His Royal Highness and those admitted to his intimacy was such, as to make it a matter of wonder that such scandalous scenes of debauchery could be permitted in a country like ours. Indeed, his acquaintance with the Prince ruined Lord Barrymore both in mind, body, and estate. While participating in the Regent's excesses, he had bound himself to do his bidding, however palpably iniquitous it might be ; and when he was discarded, in accordance with that Prince's habit of treating his favourites, he left Carlton House ruined in health and reputation.

Lord Barrymore during his last years was a martyr to the gout and other diseases ; and on his deathbed he was haunted by the recollection of what he had been, and the thought of what he might have become : indeed, the last scene of his profligate life, when tortured by the inward reproaches of his accusing conscience, was harrowing in the extreme.

LORD BYRON AND DAN MACKINNON.—During Lord Byron's sojourn at Lisbon, he was much amused with Dan Mackinnon's various funny stories. Upon one occasion Dan's time was entirely taken up by presenting women with toothbrushes, a supply of which he had received by the packet from London. Opposite his quarters there lived two very pretty Portuguese ladies, who, unmindful of Dan's proximity, and of the fact that his windows commanded a view of their chamber, dressed, undressed, and went through their morning ablutions and toilet. Dan's astonishment was great when he perceived that the fair ones never brushed their teeth ; and he lost no time in sending his servant with two tooth-brushes in paper, well perfumed and sealed up. The ladies opened the packet, and appeared delighted with the present; but judge of Mackinnon's horror in beholding those dainty creatures perseveringly brushing their raven locks with the tiny brushes !

Lord Byron was a great admirer of well-formed hands : he preferred a pretty hand to a pretty face. He was asked whether he admired pretty feet : his answer was, "that he never went so low ; " "and as for teeth," said he, " a blackamoor has as white a set of teeth as the fairest lady in the land." His Lordship added, " A Frenchman thinks very little of the teeth, face, or colour of the hair ; provided a woman put on her cashmere veil in a graceful manner and is well shod, then he is in raptures with her."

Dan Mackinnon was ever in good spirits and

good humour, and he was a great swell both in Lisbon and London. His calm smile, black eyes, and splendid figure, when he strutted in uniform down St James's Street, struck every one with admiration. He was the most active man I ever saw : he would run, jump, and climb against the most expert professional gymnasts.

CARICATURE ON THE ALLIED SOVEREIGNS.—I re-collect a droll caricature in Paris, which created much amusement among the crowds that thronged the Boulevards. It represented the Emperor of Austria seated in a magnificent carriage, with the Emperor of Russia on the box as coachman, the Prince Regent of England as postilion, and the King of Prussia as footman. The Emperor Napoleon was portrayed as a running footman, holding the handle of the carriage door, and saying to the Emperor of Austria, then his father-in-law, "*Beau père, ils m'ont mis dehors—et moi ils m'ont mis dedans.*"

It was stated in well-informed circles, that, up to the very moment the Bourbons entered Paris, the Emperor of Austria had not the slightest idea that the dethronement of the King of Rome, and the banishment of his father, were contemplated by the allied Sovereigns. But the English declared that the Bourbons were the legitimate Royal Family of France; and by the aid of a bribe to Metternich, and the exercise of their continental influence, which was then unlimited, the claim of the son of the Emperor Napoleon was set aside.

BREGUET, THE FRENCH WATCHMAKER.—This celebrated man was greatly encouraged by the Allies in 1815. The Emperor Alexander purchased several of his unequalled watches, and the Duke of Wellington also had one which, on touching a spring at any time, struck the hour and minute. The Duke carried it for many years, and it proved of great service to him on many occasions : it cost, I was told, three hundred guineas. The Duke and Duchess of Berri, the Marquis of Londonderry, Lords Beauchamp, Chesterfield, Bruce, and many others, were also customers of Breguet ; who was, without doubt, the best and most scientific watchmaker known. I frequently visited his shop, and had many conversations with him ; and, although at that time getting old, he was full of energy and vivacity. He was not an advocate for flat watches, as he said they impeded the proper action of the wheels and could not be depended upon as time-keepers : he defied any one to make a watch so good as those made on his own principle. The prices he paid to his best workmen were enormous ; there being few to whom he could confide his watches, as so many were drunkards, and could only work a day or two in the week. He told me that he paid some of them thirty francs a day, and none less than a napoleon ; and that throughout Paris there were only fifteen or twenty able to execute the delicate work necessary for such watches as he made.

Breguet was a great encourager of merit : he used to say to his young workmen, "Don't be discouraged, or allow a failure to dishearten you ; accidents will happen, miscalculations cannot altogether be avoided : be persevering, industrious, sober, and honest." Such was the advice he gave, and he frequently enabled those in his employ who were skilful, steady, and industrious, to arrive at opulence. Breguet, besides his scientific knowledge and mechanical skill, possessed great general information. Napoleon himself, knowing his abilities, frequently went incognito to the workshop and conversed upon the improvements which he was anxious to effect in cannon and fire-arms. The Russian campaign and its disasters put an end to all projects on that score.

LABÉDOYÈRE AND THE NUMBER THIRTEEN.—In 1815 Labédoyère, one of Napoleon's aide-de-camps, paid a visit to the Malmaison prior to the fallen monarch's departure for Cherbourg. The dinner hour arrived, and when the company were seated, Queen Hortense observed that the ominous number of thirteen had assembled, and that, according to the prevalent superstition, one of them would inevitably die before the expiration of a year. Labédoyère remarked, "In all probability your Majesty's prediction will be verified in me; for the Bourbons will never forgive the part I played in joining the Emperor on his return from Elba." The dinner proceeded, and nothing more was thought of the speech; but before a year was over, poor Labédoyère's anticipations were realised : he was seized by the police, brought before a court-martial composed of legitimists, and condemned to die, for having all his life espoused one cause, and fought for it bravely.

Fouché and Carnot.—During the latter part of the reign of Louis XVIII. his majesty nominated Fouché as his Minister of Police. To propitiate the Bourbonists, this man desired many of his former friends and associates to quit France, without assigning a cause. Among those who received this unexpected *congé* was the celebrated General Carnot, who wrote the following laconic epistle to Fouché: "*Où veux tu que j'aille, traitre?*" to which the following answer was given: "*Où tu voudras, imbécile.*" Both Fouché and Carnot had voted for the death of the unpopular Louis XVI., but had subsequently served as ministers to the Emperor.

L'Enfant de Troupe.—A sergeant in the 16th Dragoons, dying suddenly, and leaving his child, a fine boy, entirely unprovided for, without any one to take care of him, the officers of the regiment interested themselves in the little fellow's welfare, and adopted him. He was brought up with great care, and received a very good education; and as he was a remarkably clever youth, and his conduct was unimpeachable, he made great progress in his studies. He became a thorough musician, and could play upon several instruments, and his aptitude for learning languages was astonishing : he could speak fluently Spanish, Portuguese, French, and German, and had a fair knowledge of almost every continental language. Having attained to the rank of sergeant in the Peninsula, on the return of the regiment to England he was sent, under the charge of an officer, to continue his military studies at Clifton House ; and he afterwards attended Colonel Peter's drill in Pimlico to learn the German method of riding (thanks to the Prince Regent's love of change in every department of the army.)

Having obtained an *entrée* into the houses of several city families, and being a remarkably clever horseman, and possessing a fine figure and good looks, he became somewhat neglectful of his military duties, passing most of his time among the citizen's wives and daughters. A young lady, the daughter of a rich merchant, fell desperately in love with him, and the end of it was that our dashing young sergeant married her privately ; absenting himself for the purpose several days from Colonel Peter's drill without leave, and when he returned it was to give himself up as a deserter. His wife, who was very beautiful, and who had returned with him, flung herself on her knees before the commanding-officer to implore pardon for her husband, who was, notwithstanding, placed under arrest; but at the court-martial held on the matter he was, on the certificates of the officers of his regiment, acquitted. His discharge was obtained with his wife's money, and he was afterwards appointed second in command of one of our Indian Irregular corps ; in which country he ended his somewhat eventful life.

INCIDENT AT A BALL AT THE BRITISH EMBASSY IN PARIS, 1816.—During the reign of the Bourbons, society was, as now, divided into two or more classes ; the nobility on the one hand, and the rich mercantile men on the other. The latter studiously copied their betters in dress, manner, and style of living ; but as a system of exclusiveness was observed, which militated against their being admitted into the best *salons*, great interest was necessary to overcome the obstacle to their admission. A beautiful woman, the wife of a rich banker, being desirous of getting an invitation to a *bal costumé* given at the British Embassy in Paris, induced Mr

James Rothschild, the great financier, to ask Lady Elizabeth Stuart, the Ambassadress, for an invitation. The *entrée* being obtained by means of a ticket obtained by stealth from Sir Charles Stuart, the lady set about choosing a costume, and decided on appearing as Diana ; but, not having been classically educated, she did not bear in mind that chastity was a distinguishing characteristic of the goddess she intended to represent. The consequence was, that her appearance was such as to lead any one, not versed in Greek mythology, to suppose that the country in which Diana hunted must have lain in some happy region near the equator, where the scantiest drapery was the most agreeable costume. The lady, with a triumphant air, that was regarded as effrontery, entered the ballroom dressed, or rather undressed, as described, and approached the British Ambassadress, who, astonished at the exhibition, turned her back, and studiously avoided compromising herself by even looking at the lady during the rest of the evening ; informing the visitors present, her friends, that the " Jew " was alone responsible for the immodest appearance of this representative of the chaste goddess.

UNKNOWN PERSONS AT A BALL AT THE BRITISH
EMBASSY, PARIS.—When the late Lord Cowley was
Ambassador in Paris, Lady Cowley, during a ball
that was being given at the Embassy, observed a
face in the crowd of visitors that she was unacquainted with; she accordingly interrogated his
Lordship's private secretary and the master of the
ceremonies, but neither could find the slightest clue
as to who the gentleman was. Mr Bulwer, perceiving her Ladyship in trouble, offered his services to
find out the name of the unknown guest, and boldly
advancing towards him, accosted him in French,
saying, "I am sent by Lady Cowley to know your
name." Whereupon the stranger replied, "Before I
gratify you with mine, perhaps you will let me know
yours; for your manner is excessively impertinent,
and you require to be made an example of." Bulwer replied, that his rank as Secretary of the Embassy
authorised him to make the inquiry, as the Ambassadress did not know him. This elicited the stranger's
name and address : he was the Marquis D——.

The following morning this nobleman called upon
me, and mentioned what had occurred the previous
evening; he swore that he would run Bulwer through
the body for the insult offered him, and requested

me to be the bearer of a challenge to the offender.
I however took upon myself the responsibility of
arranging the matter without consulting any one,
and succeeded in calming the fury of the irate Marquis ; I assured him that Bulwer was the last man
in the world intentionally to insult any one, especially a French nobleman with whom he was totally
unacquainted, and used other arguments to convince
him that no affront was intended ; thus preventing
a meeting.

During the same evening, Lady Cowley discovered another stranger, and applied to Windsor
Heneage to enlighten her respecting him. Heneage
replied, " I know one thing of him ; but that he lives
in the Rue Basse du Rampart, and sold me a silver
teapot not later than yesterday." The master of the
ceremonies was sent for, and desired to request the
silversmith to inform him how he dared appear at
the ball without an invitation. The man replied,
" But I had one : I received a ticket." " Then be
pleased to produce it," was the request of the master
of the ceremonies. " I left it on my mantelpiece,"
said the intruder. " Then go and fetch it." The
intruder departed on the errand : and it is hardly
necessary to say that he did not return.

A MUSICIAN'S REPROOF.—Among those of the fashionable world in London who patronised music, early after the peace, no one was more conspicuous than Lady Flint; whose charming concerts, given generally on Sunday at her house in Birdcage Walk, delighted all who had musical tastes and enjoyed the honour of an invitation. Among the musicians present there were Dusseck and Cramer, who played on the piano, and were accompanied by Viotti and Jarnowickz, the celebrated violin players. Lady Flint's desire to gratify her friends, however, was often frustrated by the annoying conduct of those who had no taste for music, who disturbed the enjoyment of some of the most beautiful pieces by the rattling of their cups and saucers, and the tone in which their conversation was carried on. Jarnowickz, the violin player, having upon one occasion commenced a concerto by Beethoven, accompanied by his little orchestra, consisting of Cramer, Spagnoletti, Lindley, and Dragonetti, suddenly ceased playing, and apologised for so doing by stating, that the discord caused by the tea-drinkers was such as to mar the effect of the immortal composer's music. He added, that those who thus showed that they did not understand music, would perhaps appreciate

better the piece which he was about to play,—viz.,
"God save the King," to which they would listen at
least with respect. The reproof had a good effect,
for always afterwards a complete silence reigned
during the performance.

LORD ALVANLEY.—When Alvanley was at college, he was smitten with a sudden thirst for military glory, and a pair of colours in the Coldstream
Guards, then commanded by the late Duke of York,
was given him. He became the Duke of York's bosom
friend, and this unfortunately led him to become
reckless in money matters. Upon one occasion
George Anson, afterwards General Anson, asked
Alvanley at White's if he felt disposed to join a
water party on the Thames, at which his cousin, Lord
Ellenborough, and several pretty women of fashion
would assemble. He assented, inquiring where they
were to dine. Anson replied, he never thought of
dining. "Well, never mind, Anson; I will give instructions on that head." Accordingly, he told
Gunter to supply the party with a good dinner, to
hire the largest boat on the Thames, to have it car-
peted and covered with an awning, and make it as
comfortable as possible, and to hire twelve boat-

H

men : in short, nothing was to be wanting. The *fête* succeeded to the satisfaction of all parties; but Alvanley paid Gunter two hundred guineas for his folly.

Apart from his extravagance, Alvanley, the magnificent, the witty, the famous, and chivalrous, was the idol of the clubs, and of society, from the king to the ensign of the Guards. All sorts of stories used to be told of his recklessness about money. When Lord Alvanley succeeded to his father's fortune, he inherited an income of eight thousand pounds a year ; when he died, he did not leave to his brother, who succeeded to the title, above two thousand. Armstrong, full of biting sarcasm, well knowing that the noble Lord never paid ready money for anything, asked him the price of a splendid hunter he had just purchased. " I owe Mathe Milton three hundred guineas for it," was the characteristic reply.

There is another amusing story of Alvanley's extravagance. His dinners were considered perfect, and the best in London. He had given directions to have a cold apricot tart every day throughout the year, and his *maître d'hôtel* remonstrating with him upon the expense, Alvanley replied, " Go to

Gunter's, the confectioner, and purchase all the preserved apricots, and don't plague me any more about the expense."

The great charm of Alvanley's manner was its naturalness, or *naïveté.* He was an excellent classical scholar, a good speaker, and whatever he undertook he succeeded in. He had lived in nearly every court of Europe, had a vast acquaintance with the world, and his knowledge of languages was great. When he was recommended to pay his debts, he gave a list of them to his friend "Punch" Greville, but forgot to insert one of fifty thousand pounds which he owed.

SIR ASTLEY COOPER AND THE TROOP HORSES. —Sir Astley Cooper, independently of his great skill in surgery, was a very clever and humane man. He was exceedingly fond of horses, and whenever an opportunity occurred, would operate on these animals with the same judgment and skill that he bestowed on his human patients. After the battle of Waterloo, all the wounded horses of the Household Brigade of cavalry were sold by auction. Sir Astley attended the sale, and bought twelve which he considered so severely hurt as to require

the greatest care and attention in order to effect a
cure.   Having had them conveyed, under the care
of six grooms, to his park in the country, the great
surgeon followed, and with the assistance of his
servants, commenced extracting bullets and grape-
shot from the bodies and limbs of the suffering
animals.   In a very short time after the operations
had been performed, Sir Astley let them loose in
the park ; and one morning, to his great delight, he
saw the noble animals form in line, charge, and then
retreat, and afterwards gallop about, appearing
greatly contented with the lot that had befallen
them.   These manœuvres were repeated generally
every morning, to his great satisfaction and amusement.

ITALIAN BRIGANDAGE IN 1815.—In the sober age
we now live in, when Englishmen can travel from Dan
to Beersheba almost without molestation, John Bull
hears with surprise that his friends on an excursion
in Italy, not half a mile from a populous town, were
seized by a party of brigands, and only liberated on
paying a ransom of some thousands of pounds.   In
1815, however, these occurrences were very common.   In fact, at that time both Italy and Spain

swarmed with banditti, and travellers in those
countries were generally accompanied by an escort
of cavalry when in dangerous districts.

Two English gentlemen—Lord Valletort, son of
Lord Mount-Edgecumbe, and the Hon. Mr Collyer,
only son of Lord Milsington, and heir to an immense
fortune—decided on visiting Italy. In those days
Englishmen exhibited more ostentation when travelling than they do now ; and these two young
scions of nobility proved no exception to the rule,
for they started from London carrying baggage
enough to stock a clothes-shop, and money in their
pockets sufficient to form the capital of a provincial
bank : nothing was forgotten, in short, that might
mitigate the hardships of travel. They carried all
the luxuries of Pall Mall and St James's Street with
them. Of course, they had engaged a courier ; and
as character was not so much an object as cleverness
and insolence, some of the greatest blackguards and
thieves in the world were often candidates for such
a situation ; although, from the accounts of Italian
brigandage appearing daily in the papers, the cause
of the misadventures that befell travellers was invariably traced to the couriers who accompanied
them, and who gave notice to the bandits if they

were worth robbing.   Our young friends had picked
up from the purlieus of Leicester Square one of
these fellows, to accompany them on their travels,—
an Italian, without a character as usual, but of
engaging manners.   But how men could be so
deluded as to walk into a trap in the manner these
two tourists did is incomprehensible.   However,
they embarked for the Continent provided with
baggage and money enough to tempt the brigands,
even without a courier to victimise them, and after
visiting several continental cities *en route*, at length
found themselves at Rome, where they engaged an
old palace and lived in splendour for some time,
spending their money like princes, and making
themselves the talk of the city.

At length they determined on making an excursion to the south of Italy, and ordering their baggage to be packed up, they started on their journey,
accompanied by their courier.   Immediately before
reaching Fondi, the carriage was stopped, a party of
brigands made their appearance, and our travellers,
with pistols held at their heads, were commanded
to give up all that they had.   Lord Valletort, who
was very hot-headed, made some show of resistance,
and had his brains blown out instantly ; while poor

Collyer, exasperated at the foul deed, snatched a pistol from the hands of one of the gang and shot him dead ; he was then dragged out of the carriage and brutally murdered on the way-side. It is hardly necessary to state that every article of value was taken from the persons and baggage of our murdered countrymen, and that the courier disappeared with the assassins, and was never more heard of.

This foul deed, among hosts of others, was never avenged ; for we could not then, any more than now, afford to quarrel with a nation like Italy on a personal matter. Very different would have been the conduct of France in such an emergency. A frigate would have been despatched to the scene of the outrage, and a dozen of the peasantry (who are generally either brigands or in league with banditti) would have been hanged or shot in reprisal. When Napoleon I. was in Italy, he issued orders that for every Frenchman or French soldier ill-treated or killed by brigands, a dozen villagers should be shot; and after finishing off about 700 of those pests in Italy, he established a respect for French lynch law that lasted the whole time of his occupation of that peninsula ; as soon, however, as the French left

Italy, this state of things was instantly changed, and brigandage has existed from that time up to the present : for England is held, as a power by itself, in sovereign contempt by the whole of the hordes that infest Terracina and the spots so graphically described by Washington Irving.

MADAME DE STAËL AND MR CANNING. — Madame de Staël, with all her talents and attractions, was somewhat of a toady.   At one of the Duchesse de Castris' *soirées* I witnessed a quarrel between her and Mr Canning.   Madame de Staël thought that by abusing Lord Castlereagh she would obtain favour from our great statesman ; he, however, coolly informed her that the manner in which she had spoken of his political adversary prevented him from continuing to converse with her, and then made his bow, to the surprise of those present. Madame de Staël was so angry that she actually foamed at the mouth.

THE DUCHESS OF DURAS.—The Duchess of Duras was considered a clever and witty woman.   She disliked Wellington very much, for having allowed the pictures and statues in the Louvre to be removed and sent as presents to the sovereigns among the allies. The Apollo Belvidere, which had been given to the Duke by the Pope, was once the cause of a dispute between Wellington and this high-spirited lady. On meeting him one day she inquired what he intended doing with the statue. He replied that he was going to have it packed up and sent to London. " Then," replied she, " England will possess one god the more, but one man the less." " How ?" inquired our hero. " Why," replied the lady, " she will gain in possessing the statue, but her honour and yours will be sacrificed by this piece of Vandalism." The far-famed statue however, was not sent to England.

MR AND MES GRAHAM—THEIR SOIRÉES.—In the year 1816, a Mr Graham and his wife, a pretty Sicilian lady, lived in Paris in their charming hotel in the Rue Taitbout. This gentleman, who belonged to an ancient Scotch family, went to Sicily during the continental war, where he met with his wife ; and, by the good offices of Lord and Lady William Bentinck, the young couple were introduced into the best society. Mrs Graham's *ré-unions* were considered charming. The celebrated

Prince Metternich, with his beautiful wife, Lady Oxford and her daughters, Mr and Mrs Cavendish Bradshaw, Mr and Mrs Hervey Aston, were her constant visitors ; Pozzo di Borgo, the Russian ambassador, Baron Vincent, and Alava, the Austrian and Spanish representatives, also visited the Grahams frequently.

It is remarkable that all these diplomatists had accompanied the Duke of Wellington at Waterloo, and received wounds in that terrible battle. Metternich was considered by all who knew him to be one of the most astute and witty members of the *corps diplomatique ;* but few are aware of the acuteness and sagacity evinced by Pozzo, who was the inveterate enemy of the first Napoleon. He was a Corsican by birth, and in his youth a constant playmate of the younger members of the Bonaparte family ; but when the Revolution had caused nearly all the respectable families of Corsica to quit that island, Pozzo determined to try his fortune in Russia ; where he succeeded in thwarting Napoleon's schemes in almost every instance. During the continental war he came to England, where, by his wise counsel, he prevailed upon our Cabinet to send subsidies to Russia and Germany.

Napoleon ever afterwards entertained a most violent hatred against Pozzo; and on hearing his name mentioned, he would fly into a terrible rage, and exclaim, " The fellow is a traitor : he is ever in my way : he is like the erysipelas on the body. Whatever harm he can do me he does ; and by him my brain is constantly disturbed, and my nervous system kept constantly on the rack." Pozzo was born in the same year in which Bonaparte, Wellington, and Metternich first saw the light. He died very rich, and his nephew, who married into one of the oldest families in France, succeeded to his property.

To return to the Grahams : The charming Mrs Graham was courted by all who approached her ; and such was the glow of health and cheerfulness in her countenance, that no one could be in her company long without being inspired with feelings stronger than those of friendship : yet not a word was heard against her honour. She had lived happily with her husband for forty years without being blessed with a child ; but before her husband's death, to the amazement and astonishment of all her friends and of the family doctor, she bore a son, like Sarah of old. The heir-presumptive disputed the legitimacy of the little stranger, but evidence was forthcoming to prove that all was perfectly *en règle;* and the young Scottish chieftain, who will shortly attain his majority and inherit a splendid fortune, was acknowledged as the *bonâ fide* son of the aged couple.

Mr Williams Hope and his Mistress.—This gentleman inherited on coming of age a fortune of £40,000 sterling a year from his reputed father, a Dutchman. He exhibited alternately extreme recklessness in expenditure and the stinginess of a miser. He would one day spend thousands of pounds on a ball or supper, and then keep his servants for days on cold meat and stale bread. His mistress, Mlle. Jenny Coulon, a charming actress, told me that Mr Hope, suspecting her of infidelity, breakfasted with her at her lodgings as if nothing had occurred, and on leaving said, "Oh, my dear, I wish you would give me your diamonds, that I may have them newly set." Jenny, never imagining that her lover had the remotest idea of playing her false, readily gave them to him ; and a fortnight afterwards he returned the ornaments, expressing a hope that she would be pleased with the setting. On the following day, what was Jenny's horror at receiving a visit from the jeweller, who called upon her with a bill "for taking out the diamonds and replacing them with paste." The enraged fair one applied to the police for redress, but found she had no remedy, having voluntarily relinquished all claim on the diamonds by giving them up to the donor. Yet this man has been known to portion the daughter of a lady of rank with £20,000.

How to get Invited to a Ball.—Mr Williams Hope's large fortune enabled him to give the most splendid entertainments to the *beau monde* of Paris. At his balls and parties all the notables of the city were to be seen, and no expense was spared to make them the most sumptuous entertainments then given. It was his custom, when the invitations were issued, not to open any letters till the party was over; to save him the mortification of refusing those who had not been invited.

It happened that a certain Marquis, well known in Paris, who had married the sister of a prince, was desirous of being present at one of these assemblies, and accordingly wrote, requesting the favour of an invitation for himself, his wife, and his wife's sister, the Princess de C——. Receiving no answer, the

Marquis called upon Mr Hope, who received him with his usual courtesy. The Marquis began by expressing his surprise that his letter had remained unanswered, when Mr Hope assured him that he had not received the letter in question ; explaining the custom before alluded to. This explanation, however, did not satisfy the Marquis, who observed that such a proceeding was, to say the least of it, extraordinary, as letters were generally written in expectation of their receiving an answer with the least possible delay ; and he added, "Mr Hope, by your conduct you have not only insulted me, my wife, and sister-in-law, but several of my friends. I must therefore tell you, that the first time I meet you in the Champs Elysées or the Bois de Boulogne, I will give orders to my coachman to drive against your carriage ; which insult you will naturally resent." Mr Hope replied, "I am not of your opinion as to the necessity of having my carriage injured through the awkwardness or stupidity of your coachman ; and to avoid all further altercation, I will have the honour to send you as many cards of invitation to my next ball as you may wish for yourself and friends."

The Marquis swallowed the bait, returned to his

wife, overcame the objections as to the manner in which the *entrée* was obtained, and appeared with her and his sister-in-law on the appointed evening. They were received with due honours, and when supper was announced, Mr Hope advanced towards the Princess, and offering her his arm, conducted her to the place of honour at his right hand at the supper-table. The rank of the Marquis and his sister-in-law had probably more influence than his threat in procuring for him the invitation, as the vanity and ostentation of Mr Hope were no less remarkable than his meanness and eccentricity.

MELANCHOLY RESULT OF A BALL. — At one of Mr Williams Hope's balls, the crowd of visitors was so great that many persons were obliged, on leaving the saloons, to take shelter under an archway until the arrival of their carriages. The wind, a keen north-easter, was the cause of sore throat and fever to many of the fair visitors; and of those present, a General Didier and his wife, a remarkably handsome couple, were seized with quinsy, and in eight-and-forty hours afterwards they both died, and were carried to their last resting-place at Père la

Chaise, Nantes. This lamentable event created an unusual sensation in Paris at the time, and was the theme of conversation in every quarter. When it was mentioned to a friend of mine, he coolly observed that he pitied the lady, but not the General, for it was a glorious end for a soldier to be killed by a *ball*.

A ROLAND FOR AN OLIVER.—I recollect dining at the British Embassy at Paris when Lord Stuart was Ambassador. Among those invited were Long Wellesley and the elder Cornewall. The former of these gentlemen arrived very late, and was sarcastically asked by Cornewall if he would take some cheese. Mr Wellesley replied in a good-natured manner, declining the offer, and commenced his dinner as if nothing had happened. When the finger-glasses were handed round, Mr Cornewall made use of the water in his, as one does when dressing, with a tumbler and wash-hand basin; making, of course, an extraordinary noise with his mouth. Wellesley noticing this, leant over towards Cornewall, and quietly asked him if he should send one of the servants for a piece of soap, in order that he might complete his toilet.

SIR CHARLES SHAKERLEY.—This gentleman had a great horror of a dead body. On one occasion Henry Williams and some others were stopping at his house, when, some slight difference having arisen between him and Sir Charles, the latter spoke in rather an abrupt manner. The visitors, knowing their host's antipathy, determined to pay him off by a practical joke, and accordingly came down the next morning looking very grave, and informed him that Williams was seriously ill. Shakerley hastened up stairs, and found Williams lying in bed, foaming at the mouth and rolling his eyes wildly. Sir Charles, struck with the thought that his guest might die, became alarmed, and was about to send for a conveyance to remove him; but the "dying man" found it convenient to get better. When Sir Charles left the room, Williams took from his mouth a piece of soap, with which he had imitated the froth on the mouth of a man in a fit. Sir Charles was, however, so frightened, that he never said an unkind thing to the practical joker during the remainder of his visit.

"TAKING THE BULL BY THE HORNS."—The late Lord John Churchill, prior to his appointment as equerry to the làmented Duke of Sussex, commanded a frigate of H. M. Navy in the Mediterranean. The doctor of the ship, a man of great medical experience and decision, was one day expatiating to his lordship on the efficacy of blisters, which, he stated, had cured all the sailors who had been attacked with fevers.   Lord John replied, "All this may be quite true ; but if ever you apply a blister to any part of my body, by God, doctor, I will order my ship's company to throw you overboard."   "Be it so, my Lord ; but you know I invariably take the bull by the horns," replied the medico : and the matter then dropped.

A short time afterwards, the noble captain was seized with violent headache and fever, and his pulse was very high ; the doctor, therefore, determined " *coûte que coûte* " to apply his favourite remedy. Having prepared the blister, he contrived while Lord J. slept, to place it on his chest without awakening him ; he then retired to rest, but gave orders to be called if his presence was necessary. At an early hour the following morning, he was awoke by the captain's servant, who, looking more dead than alive said, that his Lordship was very violent, foaming with rage, and calling out with all his

might, "Where 's that damned doctor." The terri-
fied medico found his patient in a state of exaspera-
tion and excitement ; but upon feeling his pulse,
ascertained that the fever had greatly abated.
Lord J., though furious at the pain he was en-
during, asked what the doctor had done to him.
and quoting the " Corsair," added,—

> "Prepare thee to reply
> Clearly and full ; I love not mystery."

" In a word, sir, what does it all mean ? I am
suffering from blisters all over my body." The
doctor, unconscious of what had occurred during
the night, opened the captain's shirt collar to look
at the effects of the blister ; but the sufferer pushed
him aside, saying, " No, doctor, it is not there ; you
will find it lower down." Lower down it certainly
was, for it was discovered, like the one mentioned
in " Tom Cringle's Log," in a very awkward place.
It had, no doubt, during the night, got rubbed off
the chest and had slipped down to a very opposite
part of the body, which was blistered severely. The
doctor, to appease the captain's anger, explained :
" I found your lordship last night in a violent fever,
and had no alternative left, but to take the bull by

the horns : the blister was placed contrary to my
orders, I confess ; but 'all's well that ends well,'
and I am happy to see your lordship so much
better."

RAGGET, OF WHITE'S CLUB.—Raggett, the well-
known club proprietor of White's, and the Roxburgh
Club in St James's Square, was a notable character
in his way.   He began life as a poor man, and
died extremely rich.   It was his custom to wait
upon the members of these clubs whenever play
was going on.   Upon one occasion at the Roxburgh,
the following gentlemen, Hervey Combe, Tippoo
Smith, Ward (the Member for London,) and Sir
John Malcolm, played at high stakes at whist ;
they sat during that night, viz., Monday, the following day and night, and only separated on Wed-
nesday morning at eleven o'clock ; indeed, the party
only broke up then owing to Hervey Combe being
obliged to attend the funeral of one of his partners
who was buried on that day.   Hervey Combe, on
looking over his card, found that he was a winner
of thirty thousand pounds from Sir John Malcolm,
and he jocularly said, "Well, Sir John, you shall
have your revenge whenever you like."   Sir John

replied, "Thank you ; another sitting of the kind will oblige me to return again to India." Hervey Combe, on settling with Raggett, pulled out of his pocket a handful of counters, which amounted to several hundred pounds, over and above the thirty thousand he had won of the baronet, and he gave them to Raggett, saying, " I give them to you for sitting so long with us, and providing us with all required." Raggett was overjoyed, and in mentioning what had occurred to one of his friends a few days afterwards, he added, " I make it a rule never to allow any of my servants to be present when gentlemen play at my clubs, for it is my invariable custom to sweep the carpet after the gambling is over, and I generally find on the floor a few counters, which pays me for the trouble of sitting up. By this means I have made a decent fortune."

THE CAFÉ TORTONI.—About the commencement of the present century, Tortoni, the centre of pleasure, gallantry, and entertainment, was opened by a Neapolitan, who came to Paris to supply the Parisians with good ice. The founder of this celebrated *café* was by name Veloni, an Italian, whose father lived with Napoleon from the period he invaded

Italy, when First Consul, down to his fall. Young Veloni brought with him his friend Tortoni, an industrious and intelligent man. Veloni died of an affection of the lungs, shortly after the *café* was opened, and left the business to Tortoni; who, by dint of care, economy, and perseverance, made his *café* renowned all over Europe. Towards the end of the first Empire, and during the return of the Bourbons, and Louis Philippe's reign, this establishment was so much in vogue that it was difficult to get an ice there; after the opera and theatres were over, the Boulevards were literally choked up by the carriages of the great people of the court and the Faubourg St Germain bringing guests to Tortoni's.

In those days clubs did not exist in Paris, consequently the gay world met there. The Duchess of Berri, with her suite, came nearly every night *incognito;* the most beautiful women Paris could boast of, old maids, dowagers, and old and young men, pouring out their sentimental twaddle, and holding up to scorn their betters, congregated here. In fact, Tortoni's became a sort of club for fashionable people; the saloons were completely monopolised by them, and became the rendezvous of all that was gay, and I regret to add, immoral.

Gunter, the eldest son of the founder of the house in Berkeley Square, arrived in Paris about this period, to learn the art of making ice; for prior to the peace, our London ices and creams were acknowledged, by the English as well as foreigners, to be detestable. In the early part of the day, Tortoni's became the rendezvous of duellists and retired officers, who congregated in great numbers to breakfast; which consisted of cold *pâtés*, game, fowl, fish, eggs, broiled kidneys, iced champagne, and liqueurs from every part of the globe.

Though Tortoni succeeded in amassing a large fortune, he suddenly became morose, and showed evident signs of insanity : in fact, he was the most unhappy man on earth. On going to bed one night, he said to the lady who superintended the management of his *café*, " It is time for me to have done with the world." The lady thought lightly of what he said, but upon quitting her apartment on the following morning, she was told by one of the waiters that Tortoni had hanged himself.

Among the prominent and singular personages who used daily to visit this *café* was the Russian Prince Tuffiakin, who was immensely rich, and perhaps the greatest epicure in Paris. When he

attained the respectable age of seventy, he fell desperately in love with a beautiful girl, named Anna
Sinclair, who was born of Scotch parents. Upon
one occasion, whilst sipping his ice, the old man
observed his adored Anna ogling a young dandy,
and a serious quarrel was the consequence; however, in course of time, a sort of truce was patched
up between the lovers. The fair Scotch girl promised never more to ogle, and the old man proposed
the following plan of reconciliation; they were both
to meet at the church of Notre Dame de Lorette,
and exchange rings at the altar, and afterwards to
leave the church arm in arm. Though Tuffiakin
was of a jealous disposition, he was nevertheless a
great libertine, for he pretended to be in love with
every pretty girl he met. He suddenly became
enamoured of a well-known *danseuse*, who was
living under the protection of an English nobleman.
The Prince, well knowing the power of his money,
boldly presented himself at the lady's house, and by
the application of an immense bribe of money and
jewels, he succeeded in obtaining the good graces of
the inconstant daughter of Terpsichore. This old
Russian *débauché* hastened his death by his excesses,
and became an idiot.

Among the English persons of note who usually met at Tortoni's, I recollect Lords Brudenell Bruce, Bingham, and Chesterfield ; also Lord Herbert, afterwards Earl of Pembroke, whom the French denominated *L'air bête :* not that the noble Lord was by any means deficient in intellect, but the envy and jealousy of the French were piqued ; for he was extremely handsome, and his equipages were the finest in Paris. Sir Henry Milmay, with his beautiful and accomplished wife, created an immense sensation. Hall Standish, who spent fabulous sums upon pictures, dinners, and balls, was a *habitué* there ; and you were sure to stumble upon the kind and excellent Tommy Garth, full of spirits and youth. Lord Stair, who was club-footed, and the most unpopular Englishman in Paris, might be seen sitting in his carriage, accompanied by two dogs, within hail of the waiters. I must not forget to mention Mr Green, an epicure of the first water, who gave excellent dinners ; and also poor Cuthbert, who died in Spain, much regretted by his old friends.

It was the custom for the great ladies who came to Tortoni's, to form their parties there ; and I recollect as if it had occurred yesterday, that upon one occasion, the Princess de Beauvau invited those who were assembled in the centre room, to meet at her hotel at midnight to dance. On our arrival, we were agreeably surprised to find Musard, Colinet, and other musicians assembled, and ready to strike up a quadrille or a waltz. The charming daughters of the Princess, the Ladies Harley, with others whom I now forget, danced with all the grace of professional performers. In those days, the Minuet, Gavotte, and Monaco were the favourite dances, and if a gentleman could muster sufficient grace and agility for any of those fashionable dances, he was sure of receiving invitations from the best houses in the Faubourg St Germain.

About the period I allude to, a young captain in one of the French regiments of hussars suddenly made his appearance at Tortoni's, the Count Walewski, a natural son of the great Napoleon's. He was remarkable for his good looks; the ladies adored him; and it must be acknowledged he was one of the finest-looking men I ever saw. Not liking a military life, Walewski retired from the hussars and adopted politics; in which sphere he soon evinced considerable talent. His friends the Ducs de Morny,

and Mouchy, the Counts Antonin and Louis de No-
ailles, the Count Montguyon, and Lavallette, met here
nearly every night. Upon one occasion, a strange
scene took place between Lavallette and Montguyon,
owing to a pretty girl, Mademoiselle D., with whom
it was said that they were both in love. Be this as
it may, "the green-eyed monster" was aroused, and
from high words, a duel was the consequence ; they
fought with swords, and Montguyon received a
wound in the arm, when the seconds interfered and
put an end to the affair.

The Revolution of 1830 was a death-blow to Tortoni's. Persons in the best society, who had during
many years been considered proud and exclusive,
now began to keep entirely aloof, and studiously
avoided going there, because of the new set which
had been formed. This *café*, nevertheless, for some
time continued to be in fashion, and the rendezvous
of persons of celebrity. Victor Hugo, Lamartine,
Sophie Gay, Alexandre Dumas, the bankers Rothschild, and the moneyed aristocracy, frequently met
there. Clubs have, however, sprung up in Paris in
every direction within a few years, and the consequence has been that Tortoni's has lost its *renommée ;*

but, nevertheless, the ices here are still considered the best in Paris.

AN INVETERATE GAMBLER.—Mr Lumsden, whose inveterate love of gambling eventually caused his ruin, was to be seen every day at Frascati's, the celebrated gambling-house kept by Mme. Dunan, where some of the most celebrated women of the *demi-monde* usually congregated. He was a martyr to the gout, and his hands and knuckles were a mass of chalk stones. He stuck to the *rouge et noir* table until everybody had left ; and while playing would take from his pocket a small slate, upon which he would rub his chalk stones until blood flowed. Having on one occasion been placed near him at the *rouge et noir* table, I ventured to expostulate with him for rubbing his knuckles against his slate. He coolly answered, " I feel relieved when I see the blood ooze out."

Mr Lumsden was remarkable for his courtly manners ; but his absence of mind was astonishing, for he would frequently ask his neighbour where he was. Crowds of men and women would congregate behind his chair, to look at " the mad Englishman," as he was called ; and his eccentricities used to amuse even the croupiers. After losing a large fortune at this den of iniquity, Mr Lumsden encountered every evil of poverty, and died in a wretched lodging in the Rue St Marc.

COLONEL SEBRIGHT OF THE GUARDS.—This gentleman was well known in London, from the commencement of the present century down to 1820, as one of the most eccentric men of the age. He stuck to the old style of corduroy knee-breeches and top-boots to the day of his death. He never— that is to say, for many years before his death—left town ; and his daily occupation was to walk from his house in Chapel Street, South Audley Street, to Hyde Park, accompanied by his wiry-haired terrier. Then he would stroll to the Guards' Club, finding fault with everything and everybody connected with the changes taking place in the dress, &c., of the army, and that of the English gentleman. From the windows of the Club he used to gaze at White's, which was opposite, and abuse the dandies, especially Brummel and Alvanley, who were his especial aversions, ejaculating,

" Damn those fellows ; they are upstarts, and fit only for the society of tailors ! "

I recollect on one occasion his dining, when on guard, with Colonel Archibald Macdonald, (who was killed afterwards at Bergen-op-Zoom,) when Brummel, Alvanley, and Pierrepoint were also of the party. These dandies were aware of the dislike he entertained for them, but nevertheless made a point of asking him to take wine. But to each invitation he replied gruffly, " Thank you ; I have already had enough of this horrid stuff, and cannot drink more." His speeches were usually of this curt description.

When Sebright went to Spain with his battalion, he left directions to have the newspapers regularly forwarded to him, and on their arrival he desired his servant to damp them ; then holding them to the fire, he would exclaim, " Why, my papers smell as if they were only printed last night." This operation was performed every day the mails arrived from England.

My gallant friend was a thorough John Bull, and an enemy to everything that was French, even to the dress of that nation. It was with difficulty that he bore the innovation of the black neckcloth, that had then just come into fashion. Upon one occasion, on entering the Guards' Club, he perceived Willoughby Cotton with a black cravat on, when he said, in a loud voice, "It is evident that the officers of the Guards are in debt to their washerwomen, or they would not wear dirty black cravats." Willoughby Cotton, feeling indignant, replied that he did not understand such impertinence. Sebright then jumped up from his chair, exclaiming, "I will not brook this language!" and left the room. Colonel Keate followed the irritable gentleman, and told him that he had brought it all on himself by his sarcastic observations; and, in short, so convinced him of his error as to cause him to shake hands with Cotton.

THE PRINCESS CHARLOTTE OF WALES.—A few months after the death of the lamented Princess Charlotte of Wales, Prince Leopold, now the King of the Belgians, went to Paris, where he lived at the Hotel des Princes, Rue Richelieu; but for a length of time he remained incognito. I was on one occasion dining in the company of his Royal Highness, who interrogated me about a shooting party at St Germain, which had taken place a day or two before. When I mentioned the number of hares we had shot, the Prince observed, " I never intend again to shoot a hare, because at Claremont, one day, when walking with my beloved wife, we heard the cries of one that had been wounded by one of the shooting party ; and so affected was she by its pitiful screams, that she begged I would not be the cause of pain to one of these animals in future."

The Duchess of Leeds used to tell an anecdote of her Royal Highness and her love of fishing. When engaged in this sport, on catching a fish the Princess used to tie a piece of ribbon round its tail and throw it back again into the water, noticing with delight that those which had not been caught attacked those decorated by her. Once, having been very successful in catching a great many, and having exhausted all her ribbon, she unpicked her bonnet and made use of its trimmings to decorate the fish she caught.

THE DUKE OF CLARENCE. — At the commencement of 1817, the Duke of Clarence, bent upon improving his pecuniary means, decided on marrying a rich heiress. The report was circulated all over England, (where it produced the most intense sensation,) that the Duke had, with the consent of his brother, the Prince Regent, actually proposed to Miss Wykeham, whose estates in Oxfordshire were large and of immense value. When the event was communicated to Queen Charlotte, his royal mother was outrageous; she flew into a violent rage, and with vehement asseverations, (either in English or German,) declared that her consent should never be given to the match. The law officers of the Crown were consulted, cabinet councils met daily, and after much discussion, ministers determined on opposing the Duke's project; notwithstanding the opinion of one of the best lawyers that "a prince of the blood-royal, being of age, and notifying his intended marriage previous to its taking place, was at liberty to marry without the consent of the king, unless the two Houses of Parliament should address the Crown against it."

The excitement among all classes was at its height, when the *Morning Post* informed the world one morning that the Duke's intended marriage was entirely "off;" H. R. H. having been prevailed upon by the Queen to forego his intentions. In this course Queen Charlotte was evidently supported by the rest of the royal family; and it was whispered

K

that, as an inducement to the Prince to behave like a good boy, the Queen, Prince Regent, and his royal sisters had subscribed a sufficient sum among themselves to pay off all H. R. H's. debts, and to provide him with an increase of income for the future.   Much amusement was caused at the clubs by a caricature of an old sailor, called " the love-sick youth."

The Duke of Clarence, together with his brothers, were in the habit of frequently dining at the table prepared for the officers who mount guard at St James's, and it was the custom for their Royal Highnesses to send in their names when they intended to honour the Colonel with their presence.   Although I was at the time very young, I recollect being present on several occasions when the Duke of Clarence honoured our mess with his presence, and the amusing anecdotes he used to relate.   He astonished Colonel Archibald Macdonald one day at table by putting the following question to him : " Colonel, are you ever under the necessity of giving ' chocolate' to your young officers ?"   The Colonel (who was afterwards killed at Bergen-op-Zoom) replied, that he did not understand what H. R. H. meant by " giving chocolate."   The Duke replied,

"Oh, I can see, Colonel, that you have not breakfasted with Sir David Dundas, for it was his invariable custom to ask such officers as had fallen
under his displeasure for breaches of military discipline to breakfast with him, in order that during
the repast, where some excellent chocolate invariably
formed one of the comestibles, the culprit should be
severely lectured, and sometimes recommended to
leave the service." Ensign " *Bacchus* " Lascelles,
who was present, a plain-spoken fellow, sang out
from the end of the table, " Your Royal Highness,
if the Colonel does not understand the meaning of
' chocolate' I do ; for only this morning I received
' goose' from the adjutant for not having sufficient powder on my hair : it is quite immaterial
whether a rowing be denominated ' chocolate' or
' goose,' for it is one and the same thing." The
royal Duke laughed heartily at the *sang froid* of
the young ensign, and ever after evinced great par-
tiality for him.

Talking of military despotism, my old friend
Upton, though an excellent man, was extremely
rigorous in enforcing attention to military regulations. Having discovered that I shirked morning
parade, he sent for me, intending to adminis-

ter a due amount of "goose." On my arriving at the Queen's Lodge, where he lived as one of the equerries, and entering his apartments, I was horrified at finding this excellent fellow lying on the floor bleeding. It appeared that he had, in a temporary absence of mind, made use of a pair of razors to pull on his boots with! Fortunately, Dr Heberden, who was on duty in attendance upon the King, was immediately sent for, and succeeded in stopping the hæmorrhage ; but he at the same time expressed his fears that lock-jaw would ensue. Luckily, Upton's strong constitution carried him through the disaster, and in a few weeks he was able to resume command of the battalion : and ready to administer a plentiful allowance of "goose" to the first unlucky wight who fell under his displeasure.

THE ORIGIN OF "SHOCKING BAD HAT."—At Newmarket, when the Duke of York, surrounded by the Dukes of Queensberry, Grafton, Rutland, Portland, and other noblemen and gentlemen, was busily engaged talking about and betting on a race which was about to be run, a little insignificant-looking man pushed his head into the ring, offering to bet a considerable sum against a horse in the race in question. The Duke of York's curiosity was aroused, and he asked his neighbour who it was that offered to lay the odds. Some one cried out, " Oh, it is Walpole." " Then the little man *wears a shocking bad hat—a shocking bad hat,"* rejoined His Royal Highness. The late Lord Walpole and his father were both addicted to wearing hats with large brims and low crowns, which made the wearers appear anything but " *comme il faut."*

ENGLISHMEN IN PARIS IN 1817.—In the year 1817, Lord A———, his brother, and another friend, were staying in Paris. They had dined one day at Véry's, then the famous *restaurant* in the Palais Royal, and the conversation had turned upon the insults offered by the Parisians, particularly the military, to the English visitors. His Lordship was silent during this conversation, but took note of what had been said, while imbibing some potent Burgundy; and his indignation was none the weaker for having thus " bottled it up." On leaving the *restaurant* the first thing he did was to kick over a basket of toothpicks, which were presented to him for purchase ; the next was to shove off the pavement a Frenchman, who proved to be an officer. Of course, there was a violent altercation; cards were exchanged, and each party went his way to make arrangements for the "pistols and coffee for four."

Our countrymen, when near home, picked up their friend Manners, who had been shut out of his lodgings, and promised to accommodate him with a sofa at their rooms. On their arrival, he partially uncased and wrapped himself up in a large Witney blanket and greatcoat, and then "turned in." At an early hour the next morning, two gentlemen called on our countrymen, and were ushered into the saloon. The first who presented himself to receive them was his Lordship, who had nothing on but a large pair of trousers, and a cotton night-cap full of holes: he being so particular about having it aired that it was constantly singed in the process. Not speaking French, he requested his servant to act as interpreter, and asked the strangers the object of their visit; the incidents of the preceding night having passed off from his memory with the fumes of the Chambertin. The discussion that ensued woke up Manners, who, wrapped in his blanket, rose from his couch, looking more like a white bear than anything else. It also drew from his dormitory Captain Meade, who made his appearance from a side door, clothed only in his night-shirt and a pair of expansive Russia duck trousers, whistling, as was his wont, and spitting occasionally through a hole that had been bored in one of his front teeth, in imitation of the stage-coachmen of the day. Lord A———'s brother next appeared on the scene, in a costume little more complete than those of the others.

The visitors, although astonished at the appearance of the group, proceeded to business. Manners conducted it on the part of his friends, who could not speak French ; and, with a view of discharging his office more comfortably, drew aside the folds of his Witney blanket and placed his back against the mantelpiece, to enjoy the warmth of the glowing wood-ashes in the grate below. The Frenchmen were refused an apology by our friends, coupled with the observation, that with Englishmen the case would be different ; but that it was impossible on the present occasion to arrange matters in that way. They therefore requested the other party to name their weapons. Manners coolly informed them that they had decided on using *fusils*, at twelve paces ! This seemed rather to astonish the Frenchmen : they exchanged glances, and then cast their eyes round the room, and on the strange figures before them. Meade was whistling through his teeth; Lord A——, whose coppers were rather hot, had thrust his head out into the street through a pane of glass that had been smashed the night before; while the others were stalking about the room in their rather airy costumes. The gravity of the Frenchmen was overcome by the ludicrous aspect and *sang froid* of their opponents, and they burst out laughing. Lord A——, who was as full of fun as he was of pluck, stretching out his hand to the injured party, said, " Come, I see you are good fellows, so shake hands. I had taken rather too much wine last night." I need not say that the proffered hand was accepted, and the French officers retired. After their departure, Manners asked the servant what *fusil* really meant, as, when naming the weapon to be used, he supposed it to be a kind of pistol.

THE BOLD WIFE OF A RASH HUSBAND.—About thirty years back a bet was made in Paris by the Comte de Chatauvillard, that he would ride a horse which no groom would venture to mount because of its vicious propensities. The animal in question had been allowed to remain idle for several months, without having ever been touched by any one during all that time ; for it was fed through a hole in a neighbouring stall, and watered and littered in a similar manner. As the time approached for the conditions of the bet to be carried out, great excitement prevailed in the clubs with regard to it, especially among those skilled in horsemanship, and a wager of 20,000 francs was jointly laid by several gentlemen against the Count. Information was, however, conveyed to the Count's wife, an Irish lady by birth, and foreseeing the danger her husband would inevitably incur, she armed herself with a brace of pistols, entered the stable, and placing one of them to the horse's head, fired. The animal reared and fell dead, the lady exclaiming, " Thank God, I have done my duty ! "

A MISHAP AT ALMACK'S.—Among the many droll incidents which occurred at those elegant balls at Almack's, I recollect one which created much amusement among those who witnessed it, at the expense of the person whose name I am about to mention. The late Lord Graves, who was extremely fat, but who danced well for his size, engaged the beautiful Lady Harriet Butler one evening as his partner in a quadrille. Her Ladyship had just arrived from Paris, where she had been brought up under the auspices of Josephine, and having received lessons in dancing from the celebrated Vestris, she electrified the English with the graceful ease with which she made her *entrechats;* so much so, that a circle was generally formed to admire her dancing. Lord Graves, desirous of doing his utmost to please his fair partner, ventured on imitating the lady's *entrechat;* but in making the attempt, he unluckily fell heavily on the floor. Nothing daunted, however, he got on his legs again and finished the quadrille as well as he could ; when his friends hastened to sympathise with him. But Sir John Burke, in a sarcastic manner said, " What could have induced you, at your age and in your state, to make so great a fool of yourself as to attempt an *entrechat?* " Lord Graves not relishing the manner in which the Baronet had addressed him, replied, " If you think I am too old to dance, I consider myself not too old to blow your brains out for your impertinence ; so the sooner you find a second the better." Lord Sefton, who overheard the conversation, said, " Tut tut tut, man, the sooner you shake hands the better ; for the fact is, the world will condemn you both if you fight on such slight grounds : and you, Graves, wont have a' leg to stand on." This sensible remark led to the parties shaking hands, and thus the matter dropped.

SIR ASTLEY COOPER.—I recollect meeting this celebrated surgeon in South Wales about thirty years back, when on a visit to some of his friends. I had only returned the day before from Paris, and Sir Astley was very inquisitive about everything I had seen there. He eulogised the French surgeons, but objected to the means employed after amputation ; for instead of giving beafsteaks, port wine, and other stimulants, the French surgeons recommended lemonade and tisanes, whereby eight patients out of ten died, whereas by the English system only two succumbed out of ten. Nevertheless, he spoke of Dupuytren in the most enthusiastic terms, and acknowledged him to be the most skilful surgeon in Europe. I asked him his opinion of French cookery ; he replied, " It suits the French ; but it would never do in England ; for our men require animal food twice a-day, and porter ; but the French, from their birth, live upon fruit and vegetables, and their meat is boiled down to rags ; this is, however, congenial to their stomachs, and proves that digestion begins in the kitchen."

Our great surgeon perceiving that I was fond of smoking, cautioned me against that habit, telling me it would sooner or later be the cause of my death. If Sir Astley were now alive he would find everybody with a cigar in his mouth : men smoke now-a-days whilst they are occupied in working or hunting, riding in carriages, or otherwise employed.   During the experience of a long life, however, I never knew but one person to whom it was said that smoking was the cause of his death : he was the son of an Irish earl, and an *attaché* at our Embassy in Paris. But, alas, I have known thousands who have been carried off owing to their love of the bottle ; ay, some of the noblest and famous men in our land, splendid in youth, strength, and agility.   I regret to add, I have met with refined ladies, too, who never went to bed without a little brandy "to drive away the colic."

LADY HOLLAND AND "THE BRIDGE."—When Holland House was the rendezvous of all that was great and illustrious, a gentleman, well-known on account of his literary attainments, requested permission from its noble hostess to introduce a friend of his, who had just written a novel, which had been well received by the public. Lady Holland, ever happy to do a good-natured act, said, "You may bring him here to-night." The gentleman and his friend accordingly made their appearance that very evening, and were graciously received. On the following day, the introducer called on her ladyship to thank her for the honour she had conferred upon his friend, when she observed, "I can't say much for his good looks, for it was impossible for me to get over the bridge." "What bridge, my Lady?" "Why, the broken bridge of his nose, which has made him the ugliest man I ever saw." "Oh, madam, allow me to state that he was born with that unfortunate defect." "More's the pity, sir; and I conjure you never bring any more of your friends to Holland House who are not blessed with bridges to their noses."

THE BISHOP OF EXETER AND HIS SON.—The Bishop of Exeter, in the course of conversation at a dinner party, mentioned that many years since, while trout-fishing, he lost his watch and chain, which he supposed had been pulled from his pocket by the bough of a tree. Sometime afterwards, when staying in the same neighbourhood, he took a stroll by the side of the river, and came to the secluded spot where he supposed he had lost his valuables, and there, to his surprise and delight, he found them under a bush. The anecdote vouched for by the word of a bishop astonished the company; but this was changed to amusement by his son's inquiring, whether the watch, when found, was going. "No," replied the bishop; "the wonder was that it was not gone."

Lord Deerhurst, (afterwards Lord Coventry.)—Persons are still living who remember this nobleman hastening down Piccadilly after some pretty girl or other. Lord Deerhurst was distinguished for his good looks and manly bearing; but he always seemed in a hurry: his habits and appearance were in other respects singular, though they did not lessen the respect his rank and abilities deservedly commanded. His wit was proverbial: in short, such were his talents in society, that he was considered a match for Alvanley.

Another good trait in his character was the attention he paid to Lord Coventry, who was blind.

His marriage proved a very unhappy one. After
living some time with his wife on very bad terms,
a separation ensued, which caused him great misery.
I recollect, after this occurrence, seeing a letter
dated from his father's place in Worcestershire, in
which he said, " Here I am at leisure, free to indulge in my grief, and to correct those errors that
have brought upon me so much mental suffering."
He never completely recovered, and contrived to
kill time by travelling from London to his seat in
Worcestershire and back, once a week. Before his
death poor Deerhurst became excessively irritable,
and subsequently insane. He recovered his reason
slightly, but died shortly after, attended only by a
few trusty servants.

I recollect dining at Madame Vestris's pretty house
in St John's Wood, in company with him, Lords Alvanley and Foley, and Tom Duncombe. Deerhurst
was the life and soul of the party ; and although
there was, of course, a little sparring between him and
Alvanley, he was " cock of the walk." He was then
in good health and spirits, and conversed easily, and
without appearing conscious that he was delighting

us all with his witty sayings. Of all the dinners
I have been present at, I recollect this as being the
most pleasant ; it might be called a dinner of
dandies, as most of those present belonged to
White's, and led the *beau monde* at that period.
Of Madame Vestris I can only say, that I never
knew any lady more perfectly natural and agreeable in manner and conversation, and she did the
honours of her house in admirable style.

MR NEELD.—Lord Alvanley having been invited
to dine in Grosvenor Square, at the house of Mr
Neeld, the heir to Mr Rundell the wealthy gold-
smith, was, previous to sitting down to table, shown
some fine pictures which hung on the walls of the
drawing-room, together with many articles of *virtù*
that crowded the apartment ; the host praising
and describing each, and stating the cost, in by
no means a well-bred manner. One would have
thought that the infliction would have been dis-
continued on entering the dining-room ; but, on
the guests being seated, Mr Neeld began excusing
himself for not having a haunch of venison for
dinner, and assured his guests that a very fine
haunch of Welsh mutton had been prepared for

them. He then returned to his favourite topic, and began praising the room in which they were dining, and the furniture ; he had got to the gilding, which he assured his guests had been done by French artists at an enormous expense, when the mutton made its appearance. Lord Alvanley, who had been intensely bored, exclaimed, " I care not what your gilding cost ; but, what is more to the purpose, I am most anxious to make a trial of your *carving*, Mr Neeld, for I am excessively hungry, and should like to attack the representative of the haunch of venison."

The *nouveau riche*, though rather astonished by this remark, was obliged to let it pass without notice ; his anxiety to form a circle of aristocratic acquaintances preventing his taking offence at anything said by such a person as his Lordship.

Mrs Beaumont.—There are probably many persons who remember this lady. She was reported to have been of low origin, but inheriting vast estates in the north, and having married a colonel of militia, who became member for the county where her large estates lay, she became one of the leaders of the fashionable world in 1812. From

L

that time to 1820, it was impossible, during the London season, to walk from St James's Street to Hyde Park at a certain hour in the afternoon, without seeing her and her daughters in her large yellow landau. Her style of living was most luxurious and full of ostentation. Her preference of a nobleman before a gentleman of no title was shown in a manner that was perfectly ridiculous, and evinced a great want of good sense and tact. Her *fêtes* were thronged with the *grand monde*, and her system of excluding all but persons of rank amused the fashionable world : even men of talent and good family rarely got the *entrée* of her saloons.

This recalls to my mind a rather ludicrous incident. Through the kindness of the Duchess of Marlborough, I was present at one of Mrs Beaumont's balls, and this led to my being invited to the rest of them during the season. In fine, I became a constant visitor at her house in Portman Square, till one day I ventured to ask for an invitation for a friend of mine, a distinguished officer in the Guards, good-looking, and in every respect fit company for the best saloons. I was of course asked what was his rank ; and on my replying that he was a captain in the regiment in which I

had the honour to serve, Mrs Beaumont exclaimed,
" I want no more captains at my balls : you should
consider yourself lucky in getting an invitation." I
bowed and took my leave ; and, reflecting on the
injustice I had done Mrs Beaumont in presuming
to appear at her assemblies, I never again perpetrated the offence.

Mrs Beaumont had three sons, two of whom died
insane ; the other sorely wounded her pride by
marrying Miss Atkinson, the daughter of a hatter.
When his mother died he succeeded to her large
property, and this somewhat turned his head. Like'
all *parvenus*, he was ambitious of being raised to
the peerage ; but he threw away the only chance
he had, by quarrelling with the only great man
likely to forward his views—the celebrated Lord
Grey. Mr Wentworth Beaumont fought a duel
with the late Lord Durham, and had to pay his
second an annuity for life,—why or wherefore no
one could tell. The issue of his marriage was a
son, of whom he was very proud. Soon after the
birth of his heir, poor Beaumont became in a measure insane ; but there was method (or satire) in
his madness, for in his last moments he ejaculated,
" I cannot say that I have lived for nothing, for my

son, besides inheriting my vast fortune, will become the ' Duc de Feltre.' "

In spite of all the anxiety and trouble Mrs Beaumont had taken in bringing up her daughters, in the hope of their marrying men of exalted rank, she had the mortification of knowing that they had married men of low origin in Italy.

WINDSOR CASTLE IN 1819.—While on duty with my regiment at Windsor in the summer of 1819, I received an invitation to dine at the Equerries' table at the Castle, or the " Queen's House," as it was then called, on which occasion I met Lord Liverpool, the Prime Minister, the Archbishop of York, Dr Baillie, Sir H. Halford, Dr Heberden, and the " mad Doctor " Willis. These personages had come from London, in virtue of their office, to inquire after the health of the King. I must confess to a feeling of aversion, and even horror, at being placed next the " mad Doctor " at table. He was sallow, ill-looking, and indeed had a most forbidding countenance. He was dressed in black, with silk breeches, white neckcloth, and frill. However, my feelings were soon calmed ; for, although he never spoke, he seemed to enjoy his dinner, eating and drinking as much as any two persons at table.   Dr Baillie was evidently a great favourite with the Prime Minister and Archbishop.   The equerries present were Generals Garth and Gwynne, both fine gentlemen of the old school, in powder and pigtails.

I once saw George III. walking with his favourite son, the Duke of York, with whom he talked incessantly, repeating his, " Yes, yes, yes, Frederick," in his usual loud voice.   His beard was of unusual length, and he stooped very much.   He wore the Windsor uniform, with a large cocked hat, something like that with which Frederick the Great is usually represented. The doctors walked behind the King, which seemed greatly to annoy him, as he was constantly looking round.   It was said, and I believe with truth, that the poor King could not hear Dr Willis's name spoken without shuddering.   H. R. H. the Duke of Cumberland frequently visited his Royal parents, with his beautiful wife, whose figure at that time was such as few women could boast of.

I cannot pass by an event which caused some scandal at the time.   The Duke of Cumberland, on his visits to Windsor, was generally accompanied by his aide-de-camp, Colonel Disney.   One day, on the occasion of the Duke's recovery from the wounds received in resisting the murderous attack of his valet, H. R. H. arrived at the castle to pay his respects to his Royal parents; when, finding that the Queen was walking on the terrace, he hastened to join her Majesty, desiring Colonel Disney to remain in waiting. The Colonel, who was a harebrained, half-cracked sort of a fellow, finding waiting rather irksome, commenced making a tour through the apartments, and in his peregrinations entered her Majesty's bed-chamber, which was rightly held to be sacred ground. Curiosity led him to inspect the various toilet articles of the queen, and still further to examine a golden vase, which he put to a use that cannot be named to ears polite. This breach of good manners was detected by the royal housekeeper, the Hon. Miss Townshend, who, with tears in her eyes, reported to the Duke of Cumberland the gross impropriety. His Royal Highness, a proud overbearing man, sought out Disney, and attempted to inflict summary chastisement for the insult he had perpetrated; however, the Colonel evaded the punishment so richly deserved, but he was almost immediately placed on the shelf, and died at his lodgings, in Bury Street, St James's, heart-broken, on the second anniversary of his thoughtless freak.

A SHOULDER OF MUTTON À LA SOUBISE.—When George IV. passed through Carmarthenshire on his return from Ireland, he remained a day and night at Dynevor Castle, the seat of the nobleman of that name. His Lordship, desirous of entertaining his Majesty in a befitting manner, asked Sir Benjamin Bloomfield what particular dish the King preferred. Sir Benjamin replied, that his Majesty was very fond of a shoulder of mutton boiled with "*sauce soubise.*" Lord D. sent word to that effect to the cook, who full of vanity and self-conceit, like the majority of Welshmen, did not deign to make the inquiry as to what a "*sauce soubise*" meant. The consequence was that Taffy got into a scrape, for when the shoulder appeared on the dinner-table, the King observing it, said that he had never seen a shoulder of mutton covered with currant-jelly, instead of onion sauce. The Welch cook was called, and Lord Dynevor asked him what could have induced him to make such an egregious mistake. He replied, that he thought the gentleman (meaning the king) would prefer *sweet* sauce to that ordered by his Lordship.

ATTEMPT TO ASSASSINATE THE PRINCE REGENT.— An attempt was made to assassinate the Prince Regent when on his way home from the Houses of Parliament in 1819 ; but it happily failed. In the park, opposite Marlborough House, a bullet was fired from an air-gun by a man concealed in one of the trees, who escaped. This occurred when I was on duty at the Horse Guards, marching across the park with what was commonly called the "Tilt Guard," and I remember it was anything but pleasant to get through the mob of blackguards who were ripe for mischief. The Life Guards, who escorted the Prince Regent, evinced great want of energy on the occasion. The officer commanding the troop, when he saw the danger, should have commanded his men to charge and clear the way. Such was my opinion then ; and I am persuaded, from all that I have witnessed abroad since, that the wisest plan upon such occasions, is to take the initiative and act promptly. The fact of this attempt having been made, was doubted at the time by the public at large, but I can speak from my personal knowledge that a shot was fired, and it was aimed at the royal carriage.

CORONATION OF GEORGE IV.—At this gorgeous solemnity it fell to my lot to be on guard on the platform along which the royal procession had to pass, in order to reach the Abbey. The crowd that had congregated in this locality exceeded anything I had ever before seen : struggling, fighting, shriek- ing, and laughing, were the order of the day among this motley assemblage. Little Townsend, the chief police officer of Bow Street, with his flaxen wig and broad-brimmed hat, was to be seen hurrying from one end of the platform to the other, assuming immense importance. On the approach of the *cortège* you heard this officious person, " dressed with a little brief authority," hallooing with all his might, " Gentlemen and ladies, take care of your pockets, for you are surrounded by thieves ; " and hearty laughter responded to Mr Townsend's salutary advice.

When the procession was seen to approach, and the royal canopy came in sight, those below the plat- form were straining with all their might to get a peep at the Sovereign, and the confusion at this moment can be better imagined than described. The pick-pockets, of course, had availed themselves of the confusion, and in the twinkling of an eye there were more watches and purses snatched from the pockets of his majesty's loyal subjects than perhaps on any previous occasion.

Amidst the crowd a respectable gentleman from the Principality hallooed out in his provincial tongue, " Mr Townsend, Mr Townsend, I have been robbed of my gold watch and purse, containing all my money. What am I to do ? what am I to do to get home ? I have come two hundred miles to see this sight, and instead of receiving satisfaction ór hospitality, I am robbed by those cut-throats called ' the swell mob.' " This eloquent speech had a very different effect upon the mob than the poor Welshman had reason to expect ; for all of a sudden the refrain of the song of " Sweet Home " was shouted by a thousand voices ; and the mob bawled out, " Go back to your goats, my good fellow." The indignities that were heaped upon this unfortunate gentleman during the royal procession, and his appearance after the King had passed, created pity in the minds of all honest persons who witnessed this disgusting scene : his hat was beaten over his eyes, and his coat, neckcloth, &c., were torn off his body. For there were no police in those days ; and with the exception of a few constables and some soldiers, there was no force to prevent the metropolis from being burnt to the ground, if it had pleased the mob to have set it on fire.

GEORGE IV. AND BISHOP PORTEOUS. — Lord Brougham, the late lamented Thackeray, and others, have been very severe in their censures on the character of George IV. My readers will perhaps be interested in hearing the following :—Some few years before the death of the King, Dr Porteous, then Bishop of London, having heard that his Majesty had appointed a review of the Household Troops to take place on a Sunday, ordered his carriage, though he was in a precarious state of health, and waited upon his Majesty at Carlton House. The Bishop was most graciously received, and proceeded to say, "I am come to warn your Majesty of the awful consequences of your breaking the Sabbath, by holding a review on that day which the Almighty has hallowed and set apart for Himself." The King upon this burst into tears, and fell on his knees before the Bishop, who bestowed upon his Majesty his blessing. The King then assured Dr Porteus that no review should take place on the Sabbath during his life. Bishop Porteus then left the royal presence never more to return ; for on arriving at his residence he took to his bed, and died shortly afterwards. The King was so deeply afflicted at the news that, on hearing it, he retired into his own apartments and was heard to sob as one in deep affliction.

LATTER DAYS OF GEORGE IV.—For some months prior to his death, the King abstained from eating animal food, and lived on vegetables and pastry, for which he had a great liking. His conduct, from being that of a sensual, greedy old man, became that of a spoilt child ; and the way he spent his time was frivolous in the extreme. He was very fond of punch, made from a recipe by his *maître d'hôtel,* Mr Maddison, and which he drank after dinner ; this was the only time he was agreeable, and on these occasions he would sing songs, relate anecdotes of his youth, and play on the violoncello : afterwards going to bed in a "comfortable" state. But a nervous disorder which affected him prevented his sleeping well, and he invariably rose in the morning in the most unamiable of tempers. Poor man, he was greatly to be pitied; for he was surrounded by a set of harpies, only intent on what they could get out of him, among the most prominent of whom was Lady C——, the "English Pompadour." Sir Benjamin Bloomfield was not a favourite with this lady, and, at the first opportunity she found, she caused the King to give him his dismissal; replacing him by a tool of her own, Sir William Knighton.

DEATH AND FUNERAL OF THE DUKE OF YORK.— I perfectly recollect the sorrow felt in London at the death of the Duke of York, and the splendid funereal honours paid to him. The royal Duke died after three or four weeks suffering from dropsy, in his sixty-fourth year. His administration at the Horse Guards will long be held in remembrance, as beneficial in the highest degree to the British soldier; and such was his popularity, that ministers, statesmen, and general officers followed his remains to the grave. I recollect my late lamented friend, John Scott, telling me that his father, Lord Eldon, spoilt a new hat by placing it on the ground and putting his feet into it to keep them warm; for it was intensely cold weather at the time, and the

funeral took place at night. It is certain that a
great many persons who took part in the procession
caught severe colds from their not having sufficiently wrapped themselves up; and among them
was Mr Canning, who never entirely recovered : he
died the same year, in the room at Chiswick where
Charles James Fox breathed his last.

COLONEL THE HONOURABLE H. STANHOPE.—Next
to the death of the Duke of York, there was no
event which pained the Grenadier Guards so much
as the untimely death of the Honourable Colonel
Stanhope. He had seen much service ; served as
aide-de-camp to Sir John Moore and to Lord Lyne-
doch, and distinguished himself greatly at Waterloo.
He was the only one of the staff accompanying the
Duke of Wellington when the Duke took refuge in
our square from the enemy's cavalry, as related in
my first volume.

The sensation the death of Colonel Stanhope
created in the public mind was partly due to the
melancholy circumstance of his suicide. He had never
recovered from the effects of a gun-shot wound he had
received at the siege of St Sebastian, and under the
combined influences of pain and nervous depression,

he hanged himself in Caen Wood, the property of his father-in-law, the Earl of Mansfield. Besides his merits as a soldier, Colonel Stanhope was a most accomplished scholar and gentleman. In his youth he lived with his uncle, Mr Pitt, the great minister, and he entered the army at the age of sixteen.

SIR ROBERT PEEL's HAT.—A Welsh Baronet and M.P. entered the shop of Lock & Lincoln, in St James's Street to purchase a hat. The foreman could not find one sufficiently large for the Baronet's head, and stated that he only knew one person whose head was so large. "Who is that person?" asked the indignant Welshman. The foreman replied, "It is no other than the great minister, Sir Robert Peel." "Oh! oh!" exclaimed Taffy, "you make hats for that Radical, do you? Well, then, it shall never be said that you have sold me a hat. I have a horror of such men as your great ministers." And the Baronet left the shop in dudgeon, much to the wonder and astonishment of the hatter.

AN IRISH WELCOME.—During Sir Robert Peel's administration, Lord St Germains, who had been absent from his post on a visit to London, on returning to Dublin as Viceroy, was greeted at the railway station by some one in the crowd shouting, "'Tis glad we are to see your Honour back again amongst us!" This compliment having been gracefully acknowledged by a bow from his Lordship, the same voice was heard making the delicate inquiry, "But has your Honour taken a return ticket?"—a witty allusion to the instability of the ministry at the time, and a significant qualification of the original greeting.

THE PRINCE DE POIX.—During the reign of Charles X., the soldiers on duty at the garden gates of the Tuileries received strict orders to allow no one to enter. One day, however, a person of distinguished mien endeavoured to pass by one of the sentinels, who told him to go back, at the same time stating the orders that had been issued. "But," replied the intruder, "do you know who I am? I am the Prince de Poix, aide-de-camp to the King." "*Eh, sacre!*" was the answer of the soldier, "*quand vous seriez le roi des haricots, vous ne passeriez pas.*"

LADY NORMANBY'S BALL AT THE BRITISH EM-

BASSY, PARIS.—Lady Normanby once gave a brilliant *fête* in honour of the Duke and Duchess d'Aumale.   In the entrance hall of the Embassy were ranged twelve footmen in splendid liveries; the landing was a *bosquet* of rose trees, flowers filled the drawing-rooms, and enormous *jardinières* were placed in every direction; the garden walks were covered with carpets, and furnished with sofas, and a gorgeous marquée for dancing was erected in the garden.   The company was composed of the *élite* of society, and the most beautiful women England could boast of were present; much to the chagrin of the Parisians, whose admiration of the Englishwomen was intense, but mixed with envy. The supper was exquisite; and as there were not seats enough for all the company at once, it was arranged that none but ladies should sit, and consequently the men stood behind their partners during the repast.   Notwithstanding this arrangement, our Ambassadress observed a noble marquis seated in conversation with a person with whom she was unacquainted.   She asked somebody to inquire the stranger's name, &c., and the noble Lord replied, " I don't know him; but no doubt he is acquainted with Lady Normanby, or he

M

would not be here." Her Ladyship having received this answer, stated that she had never seen him before, and requested the master of the ceremonies to demand his name. He accordingly accosted the intruder, who gave his card, on which was incribed "The Baron Deldique." It was, however, subsequently discovered that this man was an impostor, and in the habit of attending balls without being known to either the host or any of the company.

LOUIS PHILIPPE'S SONS AT A MASKED BALL.—I witnessed a strange sight at one of the masked balls at the opera in Paris. A young man of herculean strength had intruded himself among a party of dancers in a quadrille, and laid violent hands on a young lady already engaged. The gentlemen of the party flew to the rescue, and for a few minutes all was confusion ; but four or five of the secret police presently appeared on the scene, and arrested the cause of the disturbance. I was surprised to observe that none of the other persons engaged in the disturbance were molested, but allowed to dance as if nothing had occurred, and on quitting the ball I determined to unravel the secret. After some trouble, I found that the party was composed of the sons of Louis Philippe and some of their friends, who were completely metamorphosed by the aid of false wigs, &c.

On my mentioning the circumstance to a friend of mine, Count D——, he said that they often disguised themselves, and appeared thus in public; and that one day during the preceding summer, after dining with them at Chantilly, the Duke de Nemours proposed a stroll, and taking out of his pocket his false wig and whiskers, said, " You, sir, have no occasion to disguise yourself ; but as it fell to my lot to be the son of a king, I am obliged to have recourse to disguise and strategy from morning till night."

Count Talleyrand Périgord's Private Theatricals. — Among the many ludicrous incidents that occurred during the reign of Louis XVIII., I recollect the following:—The Count Talleyrand Périgord having been appointed Ambassador—or, more properly speaking, minister—at Berne, determined to amuse his friends with theatrical representations; accordingly his dining-room was arranged with side-scenes, drop-scenes, and all the stage requisites, and he invited the dignitaries of Berne to witness the opening of his little theatre. The Count intended to have represented the part of a miller, and therefore ordered his *valet de chambre* to take off his coat, and to bring him some flour from the kitchen, with which to cover himself in a manner that would make the disguise appear natural. The valet obeyed his master's instructions to the letter, and, begging the Count to shut his eyes and remain motionless during the operation, the servant emptied the contents of a box of flour over his master's head. At that moment a courier arrived with the news that the Emperor Napoleon had disembarked at Fregus. This intelligence excited the diplomate to that degree that he flew out of the house, with the intention of calling upon the English minister to know whether he had received any tidings of the kind. The strange appearance in the streets of the Count covered with flour, occasioned a commotion in the quiet town of Berne. Men, women, and children followed the French minister, crying out, "Take care of him, for he is mad." In a word, it was with difficulty he got back to his hotel, where he found the company assembled and waiting for the performance which had been promised; but, alas! the nerves of the Count were so terribly disturbed that he relinquished the idea of enacting the part of the miller.

PRINCE TALLEYRAND'S OPINION OF THE DUKE OF WELLINGTON.—There are some personages who seem to gain, and others who lose, dignity and importance, when the achievements by which they acquired honours and fame are recorded in biography. The name of Wellington, by universal consent, heads the list of military commanders : he is not more distinguished for his military genius than for his sagacity and judgment. The late Prince Talleyrand, being at a dinner in London, soon after the French Revolution in 1830, was asked his opinion of the Duke of Wellington. The Prince replied :—" First, I must tell you that when the Duke of Wellington came to Paris in 1814 as English Ambassador, I was then Minister of Foreign Affairs. The skill the Duke displayed as a diplomatist was astonishing. He never indulged in that parade of mystification which is generally employed by ambassadors : watchfulness, prudence, and experience of human nature, were the only means he employed ; and it is not surprising that, by the use of these simple agencies, he acquired great influence over those with whom he was brought into contact.

"When the Emperor Napoleon returned from Elba, the Duke went to Vienna, where we (that is, the ambassadors and ministers of nearly every court of Europe) had been congregated for the last six months. On the Duke's arrival, his first question was, 'What have you done, gentlemen?' Prince Metternich replied, 'Nothing; absolutely nothing.' The Duke listened to what every one had to say, with his usual unassuming and non-chalant air; but it was evident that, while he seemed astounded at times at what he heard, he was exercising his great powers of observation and reflection. Determined not to lose a moment, he put his shoulders to the wheel, and the machinery, which had before moved so slowly, was at once put in rapid motion: in the incredibly short period of three days everything was arranged and finished, to the wonder and satisfaction of all his colleagues.

"After the battle of Waterloo, the illustrious Duke returned to Paris, where he had frequent opportunities of communicating with me, and, on the return of the King, I occupied my old post, that of Minister for Foreign Affairs. I was then more than ever convinced that the man who had fathomed the designs of all the cabinets of Europe was an extraordinary statesman. I discovered that, while others found everything impracticable which was proposed to them, Wellington appeared never to discover a difficulty. In a word, gentlemen, if we consider him in all his relations, public and private, it can safely be said that the Duke of Wellington is the greatest man that England, or any other country, ever produced."

MOTS OF TALLEYRAND.—General Count de Girardin had a most ugly squint, and was extremely inquisitive. Upon one occasion, he asked Talleyrand, "*Comment vont les affairs, Prince?*" "*Comme vous voyez, General; tout de travers.*"

Fontaine, the architect, who built the triumphal arch in the Carrousel, placed upon it an empty car, drawn by the famous bronze Venetian horses. Talleyrand asked him, "*Qui avez vous l'intention de mettre dans le char?*" The answer was, "*L'Empereur Napoléon, comme de raison,*" upon which Talleyrand said, "*Le char l'attend.*"

General Flahault, who when young was bald, had received an invitation to dine with the Prince de Talleyrand. In the course of conversation, he expressed to the Prince a desire to present something rare to a great lady as a mark of his esteem. Talleyrand replied, "Then present her with a lock of your hair."

THE EMPEROR NICHOLAS AT THE HAGUE.—On the occasion of the late Emperor of Russia's last visit to England, he returned home *vià* the Hague, for the purpose of paying a visit to his relative the King of Holland. During the few days the Czar remained there, a levee was held by the King, in order that his Imperial Majesty might have an opportunity of seeing the flower of the Dutch aristocracy. Among those present, the Emperor singled out a remarkably tall but well-built man, who was considered the handsomest fellow in Holland, the Baron Capelli, whose right arm had been amputated, owing to a wound received in a duel. The Emperor, little imagining how the limb had been lost, approached the Baron, and inquired in what battle he had had the misfortune of losing his arm. "I lost it in a duel, your Majesty," was the cool reply. The Emperor, without a word, turned upon his heel, and said afterwards to one of his friends, " It is a pity so fine a fellow should have been sacrificed : he had better have been killed in battle."

THE PRINCE DE LIGNE.—I had the honour of being invited by the Prince de Ligne to his country seat, Bel' Œil, one of the most magnificent mansions I ever saw. In looking over the old portraits of this princely family, the Prince jocularly observed, " You have few old families in England : in other words, your nobility are mostly of modern date ; but no one will contest that you have no Lords, for they are created by every minister who holds the helm."

Speaking of the manners we English indulge in towards foreigners, the Prince told me the following anecdote :—" I was sent by the King of the Belgians to London, as Ambassador Extraordinary, to congratulate your Queen on her accession to the throne. During the period of my sojourn at your Court, diplomatic dinners were given daily. It happened that upon one occasion I was asked a question as to the state of the Belgian army, when a noble Lord,

a *ci-devant* ambassador, without the slightest pro-
vocation, made a very offensive remark to me.   I
instantly left the dinner-table to consult a friend
as to what steps ought to be taken to resent the
insult offered ; but, after thinking the matter over,
it was considered the act of a madman, and therefore, to prevent scandal, and the creation of a bad
feeling between the English and the Belgians, the
affair was allowed to drop."

It is much to be regretted that we English are
even now in the habit of regarding all foreigners in
an unfavourable light.   The vulgar brag that any
John Bull is a match for three Frenchmen, and
other extravagances of a similar description, are
becoming obsolete ; but English tourists are still
apt to disparage foreigners, and entertain the notion
that when we set foot on the Continent, a system of
cheating and extortion commences.   These and similar prejudices, arising from ignorance of the language
and usages of foreign nations, naturally create a
bad feeling towards England and Englishmen.
Foreigners say, and not without justice, that we
are pre-eminently self-conceited, boastful, and proud.

PRIDE OF A SPANISH GRANDEE.—The Marquis of

St Jago, a young Grandee of Spain, was at one time the theme of conversation in Paris, owing to his eccentric habits and the dissolute manner in which he lived. Although well born, and sufficiently educated to be selected to accompany the Spanish Ambassador to England on the occasion of our gracious Queen's Coronation, he possessed an unparalleled fondness for dissipation, and an extensive acquaintance with the class of flatterers. Moreover, an absurd idea as to his pretensions to rank induced him to wear the ribbon of the French Cross of the Legion of Honour, and although "chaffed" about it, he continued to do so ; until one day, at the Jockey Club, some one present flatly told him that he had no right whatever to the decoration then in his buttonhole : which was true. This public rebuke proved such a stunning blow to the pride of St Jago, that he returned to Madrid broken-hearted, and died there at the early age of thirty.

THE EMPEROR'S EXTRA EQUERRY.—Some persons will have perceived with surprise that an Englishman, moving in good society, should have consented to receive the appointment of extra Equerry to the Emperor of the French. The occasion of his being installed into that office was as follows :—The gentleman in question had, when at Rome, shown some civility to Prince Louis Napoleon. The gossip of the day ran, that on the Prince's elevation to the purple, some one meeting our countryman coming out of the imperial stables, recommended him to ask for General Fleury's post, as he was better qualified for an equerry than that gallant General. Our countryman, taking the hint, promptly solicited an audience of the Emperor, which being granted, he coolly made the surprising application that had been suggested to him. The Emperor endeavoured blandly to silence the aspirant to stable honours, by reminding him that he was an Englishman; but added, "If, sir, you are really in earnest, I will name you one of my extra equerries." And this offer was gratefully accepted by the gentleman in question. *Tempora mutanter!*

THE DUKE OF WELLINGTON AND LORD STRANG-FORD.—Not long before the death of the Duke of Wellington, the late Lord Strangford, on his return from Paris, was invited by the Duke to pass a few days at Walmer Castle. His Grace inquired whether, during his sojourn in the French capital, he had seen Lord Hertford; upon which Lord Strangford replied he belonged to the same club, where they frequently met. "Ah!" added the Duke, "Lord Hertford is a man of extraordinary talents. ' He deserves to be classed among those men who possess transcendent abilities. What a pity it is that he does not live more in England, and occupy his place in the House of Lords. It was only the other day," added the Duke, "that Sir Robert Peel observed, when speaking of Hertford, that he was a man of great comprehension; not only versed in the sciences, but able to animate his mass of knowledge by a bright and active imagination. In a word, if he had lived in London, instead of frittering away his time in Paris, he would have no doubt become Prime Minister of England."

MARSHAL MAGNAN'S OPINION OF BRITISH SOLDIERS.—Soon after the *Coup d'État*, it fell to my lot to hear Marshal Magnan state, in the presence of several persons who expressed a doubt of the efficiency of the British army, that he had been in the Peninsula in 1813 and 1814, and in eleven battles, but never saw the back of the British soldier. This announcement, on the part of a

Frenchman high in command, who had seen real service, completely silenced his garrulous countrymen.

MARSHAL CANROBERT REVIEWING THE BRITISH ARMY.—At Compiègne, some two or three years back, Marshal Canrobert related a fact which redounded to his credit. At a review of the British army in the Crimea, the Duke of Cambridge, who was to have inspected the troops, observing the French Marshal approaching with his staff, requested him to assist, and to take the right; whereupon the Marshal acquiesced. When they came to the drooping of the colours, Canrobert's blood thrilled in his veins at seeing the names of several of our victories over the French; however, having undertaken the task of reviewing our troops, he accomplished the arduous and painful duty imposed upon him, and went down the line without evincing the slightest emotion. When he related this incident there were several general officers present, some of whom ventured to expostulate. The Marshal said, " There is no use in expostulating and endeavouring to conceal the fact; but those victories inscribed upon the colours were won by the British troops against us."

A READY RETORT.—C. de M——, one of the most fashionable, at the same time one of the cleverest, young men of the Restoration, had the singular taste of being in love with two ladies each old enough to be his mother. The one a duchess, the other a celebrated actress. When the Duchesse de Berri asked him whether it was really true that his taste was for old women, he replied, " *Oui, Madame, je suis l'homme du siècle.*"

AN ACT OF CHARITY.—Not many years back, on a cold winter's day, an eccentric Baronet was in the shop of Mr Mitchell in Bond Street, where a few friends of his used to congregate to pick up the news of the day. On this occasion, the Baronet was boasting of his munificence, when in came Colonel de B—— of the Guards, and addressing him said, " My dear S——, I have just left our poor friend, Jack S——, in a spunging-house without a shilling in his pocket to pay for a mutton chop." " Is it possible?" exclaimed our eccentric friend. " I will go and order something for the poor fellow which shall make his heart glad." And saying this he jumped into his cab, which was waiting at the door. Colonel de B—— lost no time in calling on the poor debtor, and told him he was in

luck, as S—— had promised to do something for him.
In a short time our charitable Baronet arrived at
the spunging-house, bringing—not the good things
that a man needs in such a predicament—but a
pottle of strawberries, which he boasted he had
given two sovereigns for !

MADAME ALBONI.—About twelve years ago the
inimitable Alboni, having finished her engagement at
the Theatre des Italiens, Paris, entered into one with
the manager of the Opera at Nantes, to sing there and
at the watering-places adjacent. She left Paris dressed,
as usual, in male attire, accompanied by a lady who
passed as the wife. During the first week after their
arrival at Nantes, they lived in furnished lodgings
on the *Place Royale*, and thought of nothing but
the piano and their scales ; the incomparable singer
attracting the other occupants of the house to the
landing place, ever and anon, by the power of her
splendid voice. One day, something occurred which
created a misunderstanding between Alboni and her
friend : from high and violent words they came to
blows, and a neat " back hander " of Alboni's on the
other's nose caused blood to flow. The injured lady
ran down stairs, and implored the porter to go for

a surgeon ; but the man, alarmed for the respectability of the house, instead of obeying, went to the police and informed them what had occurred. On his returning with two policemen, Alboni and her friend were found in hysterics ; nevertheless, they were hurried off, more dead than alive, to the police office.

When the Commissary began to interrogate the lady with the bloody nose as to the origin of their quarrel and other particulars, Alboni stepped forward, and addressing the man in authority, explained that they began to quarrel about a note in a song in " La Gazza Ladra," which opera was to be given that evening. The Commissary, wondering what it all meant, asked their names, which were given by the ladies, and Alboni implored him to release them with as little delay as possible, as she had scarcely time left to dress for the theatre. The Commissary took the ladies by the hand, and conducted them to the door, saying that he was extremely sorry that his agents had acted in so precipitate a manner as to bring through the public streets two ladies of such standing, without first ascertaining that there were good reasons for their being arrested. Alboni bowed, and said she hoped

N

to see the officer that night on the stage. The invitation was readily accepted; and when the vocalist perceived him at the conclusion of the opera, she flung her arms round his neck, to the astonishment of all present.

THE DERBY OF 1865 AND FRENCH RACING—The victory gained on the 31st May 1865, on Epsom Downs, by what is technically known as the "French stable," is a proof what good blood, careful training, and good living, under the superintendence of English trainers and stable-boys and a "captain" like Grimshaw, can do for such a specimen of horseflesh as "Gladiateur;" whose pretensions to being French consist in just this, that his sire was born in France, together with his dam : but their pedigrees run through the very purest blood of English racehorses. His owner, the Comte de Lagrange, well deserves the success which has crowned his perseverance in turf matters.

Unfortunately, the French will not understand what sport really is, in the generally received acceptation of the term in England. At a French race, nine-tenths of the men go there merely because it is fashionable, and because it is a more exciting way of killing time than sitting in a club reading the newspapers ; and as for the women, it is an opportunity for showing off a " fast," but, be it confessed, a becoming toilet, and thus becomes an attraction irresistible to a Frenchwoman. Of the true spirit of the affair the French comprehend not one iota.

Since the introduction of racing into France by Sir Charles Smith,—when the races run in the *Champs de Mars* were more often won by the mounted police, who accompanied the horses from the start to the finish, than by the beautiful specimens of " thorough-breds" that were then imported, —the breeding of "blood stock" has occupied the attention of many Frenchmen, and has been attended with no small success ; for not only have our neighbours procured from us our purest bred stallions and mares, but they have secured the services of English trainers and jockeys : upon whom they will have to depend for many, many years to come.

BALLANTYNE, ROBERTS, AND COMPANY, PRINTERS, EDINBURGH.

www.ingramcontent.com/pod-product-compliance
Lightning Source LLC
Chambersburg PA
CBHW030828270326
41928CB00007B/950